1, 2, 3 JOHN

1, 2, 3 JOHN

Michael Eaton

Christian Focus Publications

ISBN 1-85792-152-6

Published in 1996 by
Christian Focus Publications Ltd.
Geanies House, Fearn, Ross-shire,
IV20 1TW, Scotland, Great Britain.

Printed and bound in Great Britain by
The Guernsey Press Co. Ltd., Vale, Guernsey, C.I.

Cover design by Donna Macleod

Contents

PREFACE

The material presented in this 'Focus on the Bible' volume has two sources. In the first place, its foundation was a compact exegesis of 1 John that I presented to the University of South Africa in 1989 in my doctoral thesis entitled *A Theology of Encouragement – A Step Towards a Non-Legalistic Soteriology*. This exegesis was, however, omitted from the published version (*A Theology of Encouragement*, Paternoster, 1995). The present work is altogether different. It has fewer footnotes by far, but the exposition is fuller, and includes 2 and 3 John. Professor Adrio Konig of the University of South Africa gave help and guidance during my doctoral research. I continue to be grateful for his encouragements during those years. At one point I have changed my mind. I no longer think 1 John 5:16,17 refers to physical death.

Secondly, this book also contains, in abridged form, my preaching on 1-3 John initially in Johannesburg, in other parts of South Africa, and in Chrisco Central Church, Kenya.

I have been grateful for previous expositors. In addition to standard works (by Bonnard, R. E. Brown, Brooke, Bruce, Bultmann, Burdick, Dodd, Findlay, Haas, Law, Marshall, Schnackenburg, Smalley, Stott, Westcott), I have considered the volumes of sermons on 1 John by D. M. Lloyd-Jones and also the sermons of Dr. R. T. Kendall. Of the latter, all except two are in print in the *Westminster Record* from March 1982 onwards; the two that are missing exist as recordings.

Each expositor has to have his own interests and his own approach. My exposition has three distinctives. Firstly, in laying my material out in points, the origin in preached messages is still visible. I hope that the lay-out in points will help preachers. Secondly, I have tried to provide an alternative to the common introspective interpretation of 1 John as 'tests of life'. Thirdly, I have tried to present the message of each section rather than get involved in minutiae of exegetical disputes, although the task of exegesis has not been omitted. The larger commentaries can be consulted for such matters. My own aim has been to provide a line of theological exposition for preachers without too many distractions.

The traditional expositions of 1 John are introspective. John Cotton, famous in connection with the 'Antinomian controversy' of the 1630s, preached through 1 John in England before his migration to America, but apparently came to understand the epistle less introspectively in later years. His exposition was published after his death, but it is not certain that he would have approved of its being published. However, the volume deserves to be more widely known despite some points where one might improve the exposition (see *An Exposition of First John*, Sovereign Grace, 1962; original 1657). Zane Hodges' exposition in the Bible Knowledge Commentary (Victor, 1984) is a pointer to a less introspective exposition.

As always I am grateful to friends and family for their encouragement of my preaching and writing.

INTRODUCTION

The modern church needs the message of 1, 2 and 3 John. When the author of these epistles looked at false teaching concerning the person of Jesus, he said 'Keep yourself from idols' and warned that a reconstructed 'Jesus' other than the Jesus who was the Son of God in the flesh could never lead to 'fellowship with the Father and the Son'. Such a message is needed today more than ever.

A further reason why 1, 2 and 3 John are needed is connected with the various revivals that are taking place in different parts of the world. Attached to these movements of renewal have been extreme claims of one kind or another. 1 John shows the way to know whether claims to spiritual experience are truly of God, and it guides us into a 'fellowship with the Father and with the Son' which is built upon Christian orthodoxy and leads to Christian love. In most of the world the old-fashioned destructive Christology is not the main problem any longer. Destructive theology concerning Jesus is always suicidal. It produces no true converts, it destroys churches, it ruins nations. The spiritual power of nineteenth- and early twentieth-century 'liberalism' was nil. Many churches in the west, having been ruined by destructive scholarship and having struggled through various reunion schemes, are now drastically depleted in numbers and influence. The numerical preponderance of Christians is in the southern hemisphere.

A new conflict is facing the churches throughout the world, not a conflict with theological liberalism, but with the need to distinguish the true and the false amidst powerful movements of God's Holy Spirit. The letters of John will help us to bury destructive heresies of an age gone by and prepare us to 'test the spirits' amidst all that God is doing today.

The authorship of 1-3 John

It seems that all three letters were written by John the apostle in his old age, while he was residing in Ephesus, capital of the Roman province of Asia. While some early Christian statements concerning 1-3 John are capable of more than one interpretation, there are no grounds for thinking that our traditions concerning these letters are mistaken.

Among early references to these letters we may leave aside phrases that seem to be echoes of 1 John in Clement of Rome (AD 90s), in the letters of Ignatius (about AD 110-115), in the *Didache* (AD 90-120?), and in the letter of Barnabas (AD 130 or thereabouts). It is uncertain whether these are allusions to 1 John or simply echoes of the kind of vocabulary that was used in early churches and also found its way into 1 John.

More clearly, Polycarp writing before AD 140 echoes 1 John 4:2 or 2 John 7 (or both), and therefore seems to have known 1 John. Papias of Hierapolis (mid-second century) knew 1 John. Irenaeus (about AD 180) attributed at least 1 and 2 John to the 'disciple of the Lord' whom he also took to be the author of the fourth gospel. The Muratorian fragment (a late second century Latin list of inspired books of the church) mentions John the apostle as author of John's gospel and two epistles. Clement of Alexandria (who died about AD 220) ascribes 1 John to the apostle John, and knows of at least one other epistle of

John. Tertullian (who died about AD 215) quotes 1 John as written by the apostle. Origen (who died in the 250s) mentions all three letters. Later still there is evidence that John the apostle was regarded as the author of 1 John.[1] The evidence concerning 2 and 3 John is less plentiful, but that is to be expected with such short and relatively less significant letters.

Our conviction about New Testament documents depend a lot on what we think of the reliability of early Christian traditions. If we think that early tradition is not reliable, then the way is left open for a great deal of speculation concerning the dates and authorship of the New Testament documents. On the other hand, if we are convinced that early traditions concerning the New Testament exhibit a high degree of accuracy and trustworthiness, then our convictions concerning the origin of our New Testament documents will be a simpler matter. If the tradition is to be trusted, the apostle John wrote 1-3 John.

It is likely that the gospel of John and these letters of John have a common authorship. There are many similarities between them, in vocabulary, doctrine and syntax.[2] C. H. Dodd[3] and others have questioned whether this is as significant as might be thought, and there are words

---

1. For this material, see further A. E. Brooke, *A Critical and Exegetical Commentary on the Johannine Epistles* (Clark, 1912), pp.lii-lxii; R. E. Brown, *The Epistles of John* (Chapman, 1983), pp.3-13.
2. See Brooke, *Epistles*, pp. i-xix, 235; R. Law, *The Tests of Life* (1914, reprinted Baker, 1979), pp. 339-363; V. Poythress, *The Use of the Intersentence Conjunctions De, Oun, Kai and Asyndeton in the Gospel of John*, NovT, 26, 1984, pp. 312-334; V. Poythress, *Testing for Johannine Authorship by Examining the Use of Conjunctions*, WTJ, 46, 1984, pp. 350-369; J. R. W. Stott, *The Epistles of John* (IVP, 1964), pp. 16-24.
3. See C.H.Dodd, *The Johannine Epistles* (Hodder, 1946), pp.xlviiff

in the gospel not found in the epistle and vice versa[4], yet the objections do not amount to much and it remains likely that the gospel and the epistle have a common author. This is not the place to discuss the authorship of John's Gospel; the early reports are virtually unanimous in attributing that gospel to John the apostle.[5] Also there are such links between 1 John and the other two letters that common authorship is widely acknowledged.

The external evidence that John the apostle wrote these letters is supported by the character of the letters themselves. 1 John 1:1-4 requires an author who was an eyewitness and contemporary of Jesus, someone so close to Jesus that he saw Him with his eyes and had occasion to touch him. The word 'we' in 1 John sometimes seems to denote eyewitness apostleship (1 John 1:1, 3; 4:14). Also the entire tone of the letter rings with apostolic authority, extending over a number of congregations.

The author of 2 and 3 John calls himself 'the elder'. Some have thought there was a second John, 'John the elder' who should be distinguished from 'John the apostle'. This idea goes back to Eusebius but, although it is possible that there were two Johns at Ephesus, it is the apostle who was known to be the author of the gospel and epistles. The use of the title 'elder' does not contradict this. When there was no need to assert apostleship, an apostle might well prefer to use a gentler expression. Peter preferred to call himself an elder in 1 Peter 5:1.

---

4. See Brooke, *Epistles*, pp. i-xix, 235-242.
5. See D. A. Carson, D. J. Moo & L. Morris, *An Introduction to the New Testament* (Apollos, 1992), pp. 135-157; D. A. Carson, *The Gospel According to John* (Eerdmans, 1990).

The Historical Situation

The letters of John almost certainly were addressed to readers in the area of Ephesus, in the Roman province of Asia. Paul worked there in the AD 50s, and 'all the inhabitants of Asia heard the word of the Lord' (Acts 19:10). The seven churches of the book of Revelation were founded at this time, with the church at nearby Colossae being founded by Paul's co-worker Epaphras.

Some years later there was a turning away from the gospel in Roman Asia. Paul warned the Ephesian elders that it would happen (Acts 20:30), and just before his death wrote 'All who are in Asia turned away from me' (2 Tim. 1:15). We have evidence that there was much 'philosophy and empty deception' in the area. Colossians 2:8 said as much and Colossae was not far from Ephesus. In the AD 60s, Paul had to give directions to Timothy at Ephesus to instruct certain people not to teach strange doctrines (1 Tim. 1:3). But towards the end of that decade help came to the Christians through the immigration there of Palestinian Christians, among whom were Philip (of Acts 21)[6] and the apostle John who made his home there. The hostility towards the gospel arose through those in the AD 60s who wished to mix pagan ideas popular in Roman Asia with the Christian faith that had started thirty years previously.

The evidence of 1 John indicates that false teachers had been attaching themselves to the churches. Those who maintain that the gospel of John and the letters of John were written by different men on different occasions,[7] tend to think that the struggle in 1 and 2 John is centred on two contrary interpretations of the 'Johannine Community'.

6. See Eusebius's *Ecclesiastical History*, 2:15:2; 3:36:2; 3:39:1-17.
7. Brown, *Epistles*, p. xi.

In this case, two groups of disciples are fighting each other
over their ideas of the Christian faith, both of them making equal claims to orthodoxy. The idea is that the
doctrine which in the end won out in the church as the
'right' doctrine was only one of various options to begin
with. Smalley is one of those who think that the distinction between heresy and orthodoxy did not exist at the
first-century stage of Christian history[8] (surely a mistaken
judgement if the New Testament is to be taken seriously).

However, the New Testament points to a different
scenario. As early as the AD 60s some forerunners of
'gnosticism' existed. 'Gnosticism' was a pagan philosophy in which matter and spirit were thought to be antago-
nistic, and in which matter was thought to be evil. The
body was disparaged. Spiritual progress (in the gnostic
view) comes by 'knowledge' pursued by an elite who have
access to some kind of hidden wisdom. Although there is
variety of emphasis in the teaching of New Testament
writings, there is also a distinction between orthodox and
heresy (though of course those precise terms are not used).
The writers of the New Testament show a basic unity in
what they say.[9] The pastoral epistles (see 1 Tim. 1:3-11),
the book of Revelation (see 2:2, 6, 15, 20, 24), 2 Peter
(see 2:1), and Jude (throughout) all focus on groups which,
to use a later word, they would have called 'heretical'. 1
and 2 John are no different in this respect. In the writings

8. S. S. Smalley, *Diversity and Development in John*, NTS, 17, 1970-
1971, pp. 276-292, developed at length in S. S. Smalley, *1,2,3 John*
(WBC; Word, 1984).
9. See A. M. Hunter, *The Unity of the New Testament* (SCM, 1943). This
little book is still of value though the discussion of 'unity and variety' in
the New Testament has developed since Hunter's days.

of Paul we read of heretical opponents very obviously in 2 Corinthians, Galatians, Philippians and Colossians, and less conspicuously elsewhere. The various writers of the New Testament would have recognised each other as fellow Christians, and did so (see Gal. 2:9), but they also recognised the existence of what was later given the name of heresy.

Although full-blown gnosticism is best known from the writings of the early church fathers, especially Irenaeus (about 180), Hippolytus (who died about 235) and Tertullian (who died about 215), yet some early versions of 'gnosticism' are referred to in Colossians, 1 Timothy and Titus. Irenaeus and Hippolytus spoke of the immense variety in later gnosticism and compared it to the many-headed creatures of Greek legend. The systems of later gnosticism do not seem to have existed in New Testament times, but just as 'gnosis', knowledge, was a key idea in later times, even in the days of the New Testament there are warnings against 'knowledge falsely so called' (1 Tim. 6:20). The idea was that there was some kind of secret 'knowledge', known only to a select group who were capable of receiving it. All forms of gnosticism were pre-occupied with the idea of elitist 'knowledge' giving an intellectualised kind of redemption to a spiritual aristocracy. 'If any one possesses *gnosis*,' says the heretical *Gospel of Truth*, 'he is a being who comes from above.'[10]

It is unlikely that this 'proto-gnosticism' ever had any kind of acceptance in the church. John says, 'They went out from us, but they were not of us' (1 John 2:19). The religion of the proto-gnostics was never the result of their

10. Nag Hammadi Codex (discovered 1946) 13:22:1.

accepting the message of the Christian church. The picture is not of two alternative interpretations of the gospel, but of a group which attached itself to the Christian church and claimed that its teaching and that of the Christian church was the same. One thinks of Galatians 2:4 ('false brothers ... who came in by subterfuge') and Jude 4 ('men have crept in unnoticed'). It is not a matter of two groups with equal rights of interpreting the gospel. It is rather one group possessing apostolic credentials and another group who were not authentic Christians. John says: 'If they had been from us, they would have remained with us, but they went out in order that it might be made clear that none of them were of us' (2:19).

It is true that the gospel of John was capable of more than one interpretation, and was later much used by the gnostics. But if 1 and 2 John were written by the apostle himself, as seems to be the case, he was the first to repudiate entirely the idea that his message could be merged with that of the proto-gnostics. By the time John writes, the 'proto-gnostics' had given up attempts to win over the churches (1 John 2:19). Yet they had apparently left an after-effect in the churches, and John writes to counter the remaining and corrupting influence of the false teachers.

Most philosophies of the ancient Mediterranean world tended to have problems in believing in the goodness of matter. This meant that they tended to dislike the idea of creation by a good God. They had problems with the notion of the resurrection of the body, and they had difficulty believing that the Son of God could genuinely take human flesh upon himself. Such philosophies are known to have been in the areas of Ephesus, and it is possible to detect in 1 John the problems that had surfaced because counterfeit 'Christians' at some stage attached themselves to the Ephesian churches.

Firstly, they clearly were docetists. 'Docetism' is the heresy that denies the reality of Jesus' human nature. It denies the eternity of Jesus (1 John 1:1), and that he was the Son of God in the flesh. John has to assert the physical reality of the Son of God (1:1-4).

Secondly, there was a gnostic element. Clearly they claimed some special knowledge. Despite the carelessness of their lives and their views concerning their having no sin, they claimed to be having very special fellowship with God, derived from elitist 'knowledge'.

Thirdly, there was an antinomian ingredient to their teaching. They played down the reality of sin. They had no grasp of God's holiness ('The message we heard ... that God is light', 1:5), yet said they were having fellowship with God. However, John could see they were 'walking in darkness' (1:6). They claimed they had no sin (1:8); perhaps they said that sin was linked with the body and could not touch those who were focusing on the 'spiritual' and not on the 'physical' side of life. They could claim that they had not actually committed any sin at all (1:10). They were not bothered about 'God's commandments' (2:3), and the love of the Christians for each other had suffered (2:5). The Christians were becoming unlike Jesus (2:6), and badly needed reminding about the 'new commandment' concerning love (2:7). There had been such breaches of love that John can call it 'hate' (2:9,11).

Fourthly, the influence of the teachers had undermined the assurance of the Christians at Ephesus. They had lost their joy (1:4) and needed the kind of assurance John gives them in 1 John 2:12-14.

Fifthly, they were opposed to John and those who had accepted John's message. Sometimes in 1 John 'We' means 'We Johannine Christians as opposed to the false teachers who are seeking to influence us'.

And sixthly, they were claiming fellowship with God, but John denies that their fellowship is real.

The visitors had done damage. John writes to reverse the entire situation and restore orthodoxy, confidence, joy and love in the churches. John wants his little children (i) to know the reality of the incarnation, (ii) to maintain real and genuine fellowship with the Father and the Son, and with each other, (iii) to be realistic about sin and yet not to be complacent about it, (iv) to experience a recovery of Christian obedience in their lives and show the love of Jesus in their fellowship, and (v) to experience a recovery of joy.

Approaches to the 'tests' of 1 John

1 John is an important letter for its teaching concerning the relationship that an incarnational understanding of Jesus has with fellowship with God and obedience. The matter is vital in our own day. However, parts of the letter have often been interpreted introspectively and legalistically as though it were urging obedience to the Mosaic law, and as though it were an invitation for individuals to decide whether or not they are truly regenerate. 1 John was not written to encourage preoccupation with the Mosaic law, and it was not written to encourage introspective worryings about whether our weak level of godliness means that we have not truly experienced God's salvation. Actually the letter never uses the term 'law' (*nomos*). 'Lawlessness' (*anomia*) occurs only infrequently and should

not be translated 'transgression of the law'. 1 John has in fact nothing to say about Mosaic institutions. The 'tests of life',[11] as they have been called, are often taken as an invitation to introspection, yet the way in which this is done must be questioned. Similarly, it has sometimes been taken for granted – without discussion – that the word 'command' (*entole*) in the Johannine writings refers to 'legal ordinances' (where it is plural) or 'a precept of the whole law' (where it is singular).[12] Is this so? The whole matter invites consideration. We shall follow John's argument and discover that it is not an introspective letter, and has nothing to say about the Mosaic law.

For example, commenting on 1 John 2:7-11, J. M. Boice recalls John 13:34, 35 and says it is only by love that the world may know that Christians are indeed Christians. But then he wants to expand this to make an additional point: 'It is only by love that *Christians* may know they are Christians.' The Christian, says Boice, 'may know that he has been truly made alive by Christ when he finds himself beginning to love and actually loving those others for whom Christ died'[13]. It is interesting that he feels free to modify what Jesus said! Jesus says *the world* needs our love in order to be convinced that Jesus' mission to the world is genuine. Of course, if we have experienced salvation in Jesus we are often conscious that our life has been changed by God. We shall know that we are what we are by the grace of God. But it is a mistaken exposition of 1 John to think we have to get assurance of salvation by love. This is close to the teaching of medieval Catholicism. It was precisely

---

11. R. Law, *The Tests of Life*, 3rd ed. 1914, reprinted Baker 1968.
12. G. S. Sloyan, *Is Christ the End of the Law?* (Westminster, 1978), p. 25.
13. J. M. Boice, *The Epistles of John* (Zondervan, 1979), p. 64.

the Reformers' point that medieval Catholicism put *love* where they should have put *faith*. Assurance of salvation does not come by introspectively evaluating the measure of our love.

It cannot be denied that it is a good thing to face seriously whether we are people of love, but not in order to decide whether we are regenerate! If we do that we shall always have doubts about our salvation. Our love is a weak feeble thing, in no way adequate to be the basis of assurance of salvation. John Cotton was right to make the point repeatedly at the time of the 'Antinomian Controversy'.[14] I have written about this matter elsewhere.[15] At the moment it must suffice to say that we shall see that John's subject concerns true and false versions of fellowship with God. It is not an invitation to introspective doubts concerning salvation.

'Knowing God' is the major theme of 1 John. It was the main matter in dispute between John and the cult that was trying to entice away his 'little children'.

The Greek verb *ginosko* ('to know') occurs 25 times: 2:3, 4, 5, 13, 14, 18, 29; 3:1, 6, 16, 19, 20, 24; 4:2, 6, 7, 8, 13, 16; 5:2, 20). The verb *oida* (another verb for 'to know') occurs 15 times: 2:11, 20, 21, 29; 3:2, 5, 14, 15; 5:13, 15, 18, 19, 20).

In Classical Greek the first verb meant 'know by experience' and the second meant 'know directly'. However, in

---

14. See R. T. Kendall, *Calvin and English Calvinism to 1649* (OUP, 1979), pp. 167-183.
15. See M. A. Eaton, *Baptism with the Spirit* (IVP, 1989), *Theology of Encouragement* (Paternoster, 1995). Paul's teaching concerning the law receives exposition in M. A. Eaton, *Living Under Grace* (Nelson Word, 1994).

the Hellenistic Greek of the New Testament, the distinction between the two verbs is not a sharp one. They overlap in connotation, and both have a wide range of meanings. When, for example, in 1 John 2:29 John switches from *oida* to *ginosko* very easily, it is not likely that there is any great change in meaning. As often in the Johannine writings, the nuances of meaning are so varied as to give rise to difficulties in interpretation.

The ancient 'gnostics' had their ideas about 'knowing God' and it is a crucial matter among modern Christians also. As one looks at the church today there seems to be one half who are having rich experiences of God, but mixed in with it is a lot of falsity, incredible weakness with regard to God's Word, and sometimes ingredients that are more in keeping with a cult than the Christian church. Yet on the other side there is a cold interest in doctrine and the teaching of 'the Word' that seem powerless. On all sides the need of the hour, as it is the need of every age of the church, is of a true and authentic knowledge of God. It is here that John helps us.

I doubt whether there are any occasions in 1 John where John's idea of 'knowing' is concerned with 'deduction by sheer reason'. Yet John's word 'know' is often taken to be virtually synonymous with 'deduce' and to refer to a deductive kind of knowledge. 'There is a form of assurance which is derived by deduction from the Scriptures' says one writer who then proceeds a few lines later to mention 1 John 3:14.[16] The early John Cotton held the same view. 1 John 3:14 enables us (thought Cotton) 'to try our own states, whether we are in death or life'. (There is reason to

---

16. D. M. Lloyd-Jones, *Romans: Sons of God*, pp. 302-303

think Cotton later changed his mind.[17]) 'Here is the proof
that ...', says the New English Bible, translating 1 John
4:13.

However, it is not likely that John is ever referring to
logical deduction. It is far more likely that the force of
the verb (*oidamen*) is 'we experience'. The word *oida*
(used in 1 John 3:14) may have this nuance. Ignatius asks
his readers at Rome to 'sympathise with me' (*sumpatheito
moi*) as those who are 'experiencing the things that con-
strain me' (*eidos ta sunechonta me*).[18] Also the phrase
contrasts with 'abiding in death'. The opposite of abiding
in death is surely experiencing life. This thought coheres
with John's teaching elsewhere. He is concerned that those
who are Christians may experience fellowship. His point
in 1 John 3:14 is, I believe, that the pathway of love is the
key to *experiencing* the fact that the Christian has passed
from death to life. To 'know' is to 'experience'.

The closest John comes to using a word meaning
'deduce' is in 1 John 2:18, which could refer to the Christian's deduction from the presence of antichrists that it is
the last hour. Yet even there it is not simply a matter of
rationalistically drawing a conclusion. It is rather that the
believers' experience of God leads them on to reflect upon
their faith at a deeper level. There is still an experiential
note in his 'deduction'.

Both *ginosko* and *oida* may mean 'know by reflection
and meditation'. When John says 'If we know that he hears
us ...', that knowledge in itself is something experiential
and given by the Spirit. The conclusion that John draws

---

17. See Kendall, *Calvinism*, p.110; C.Mather, *Magnalia Christ Ameri-
cana*, 1852, reprinted 1979, vol. l, p. 280.
18 Ignatius to *Romans 6:3*.

('Then we know...') is not simply a rationalistic deduction. It is rather a reflection upon our experience of God in such a way that the Christian discerns more than he had done at first. This means then that oftentimes the knowledge John refers to is not sheer deduction but the *knowledge that comes from deeper after-the-event reflection.* When John says 'we know that we have known him' (1 John 2:3), the second verb refers (I am suggesting) to fellowship with God, and the first verb therefore refers to a present reflection and meditation.

Sometimes the knowledge John refers to is closely related to, if not identical with, 'fellowship' with God. In such cases John uses the direct object and says 'we have known him' (*egnokamen auton*) or some similar phrase (1 John 2:3, 4,13,14; 3:6; 4:6, 7, 8; 5:20). The claim of the heretics, 'I know him' (2:4), was a claim to fellowship, although it is a claim that John denies.

Sometimes the nuance that is found in these verbs is that of *direct experiential knowledge* and the verb could be translated 'we experience'. In 1 John 2:5 'By this we know that we are in him' John is probably not inviting us to decide whether we are in fellowship by our obedience (despite many interpretations along those lines). What degree of obedience would be needed? If it is to be obedient most of the time, who decides what is most of the time? Who can ever pass the test? It is more likely that 'know that' means 'experience that'. It is obedience to the Word of God that leads to our being 'in' Jesus, that is to say, in conscious fellowship with him.

Although the precise points at which this nuance is to be seen is debateable, it is likely that it is found in 1 John 2:5; 3:14, 19, 24; 4:13,16. I shall try to show how such an

interpretation fits into the overall thrust of John's meditations. In 1 John 5:15 we have reference to a gripping conviction that God has heard the Christian ('if we know...'),
followed by a further conviction that follows from it ('...
then we know') .

In 1 John 2:11 *oida* refers to general understanding or
comprehension; 'knowledge' is the opposite of confusion.
1 John 5:20, without using a verb for 'know', refers to
being 'given understanding' (*dianoia*). The Christian
living in animosity is confused and 'does not understand'
(*ouk oiden*) his direction in life. In 1 John 2:20 'knowledge' is discernment given by the Holy Spirit. Whereas
John's enemies may claim that only an elite have understanding, John maintains that all of his disciples have
understanding. The verb is used absolutely, without an
object, but immediately afterwards John speaks of 'knowing the truth' (1 John 2:21). It is this 'discernment' that
the world does not have, and accordingly the world does
not discern the nature of the Christians (1 John 3:1).

Both *oida* and *ginosko* are used of apprehension of
particular matters concerning Jesus (1 John 2:29; 3:1) and
concerning spiritual truths that are the outworking of their
knowledge of Jesus (1 John 2:29). When John says 'we
know that ... we shall be like him', it is inner conviction
and apprehension that is in view (1 John 3:2). Likewise
the Christian 'knows' the purpose of the appearing of
Jesus (1 John 3:5). The Christian 'knows' that the spirit of
murder does not stem from eternal life (1 John 3:15).
1 John 3:16 refers to the Christian's seeing, in his understanding of the death of Jesus, what love is. 1 John 4:2,6
(second occurrence) and 5:2,13,18,19 may refer to
perceiving what is authentically of the Holy Spirit.

According to 1 John 5:15, the Christian is sometimes able to attain certainty that his prayer has been heard by God

This is John's idea of 'knowledge'. It is identical to fellowship. It is rich experience of the living God. It is knowledge that comes by reflecting prayerfully on what God has done in our lives. It flows out in love towards people. According to John, knowledge that does not flow out in love towards fellow Christians is entirely fake. The true knowledge is knowledge of God, to be found when we persist in faith in Jesus Christ, the Son of God come in the flesh.

The structure of John's first epistle
The structures of 2 and 3 John are relatively simple, but 1 John requires more attention. A number of scholars have urged that it has no structure or have despaired of producing any coherent outline of the book. For I. H. Marshall it is 'extremely difficult to find a pattern in the author's thinking'. He surveys seven outlines but finds weaknesses in them all, and concludes by suggesting there are no major sections but simply 'a series of connected paragraphs whose relation to one another is governed by association of ideas rather than by logical plan'. The epistle, he thinks, 'is not meant to be divided into large sections on a logical basis'.[19]

Certainly John's style is meditative and circular rather than argumentative and linear. Yet there is a measure of argumentation in 1 John; he is clearly arguing against what he considers to be an alien and heretical influence in the life of the churches. It is also possible to discern a gentle forward movement as his letter progresses. 1 John 1:1-4

19. Marshall, *Epistles of John*, pp. 22-27.

clearly is some kind of basis for the rest of the book. Commentators generally call it a 'Prologue'. The claims of his
opponents (or those he wants to oppose) that occur in 1:6-
2:2 clearly have a definite structure. The warning against
the 'sin unto death' comes at the end but not earlier; unlike some topics in the book it is not the subject of repeti-
tion, but functions as a final and hitherto unmentioned
warning. In the bulk of the book (2:3-5:5) three themes
constantly recur: obedience, love and truth. It is those
themes that are repeated. It may be suggested therefore
that those commentators are working along the right lines
who suggest there are 'cycles' of meditation in the central
sections of the book. J. R. W. Stott, for example, sees a
prologue followed by three sections (2:3-27; 2:28-4:6; 4:7-
5:5) each of which meditates on three tests of salvation
(as Stott calls them).[20] Then follow concluding witnesses
to the truth (5:6-17), affirmations and exhortation (5:18-21).

The minor units of I John are not so difficult to discern
as any possible major units. The *minor* units of my analysis below (1:1-4; 1:5-2:2; 2:3-6; 2:7-11; 2:12-14; 2:15-
17; 2:18-27; 2:28-3:3; 3:4-10; 3:11-18; 3:19-24; 4:1-6; 4:7-
12; 4:13-16; 4:17-21; 5:1-5; 5:6-12; 5:13-17; 5:18-21) may
be discerned without a great deal of controversy.

As one compares these *minor* units with those in other
analyses that have been suggested, it becomes apparent
that there is a large measure of agreement. I. H. Marshall
analyses 1 John into 14 units which generally are identical to the ones below. (However he combines 2:3-11, 12-
17; 4:13-5:4; 5:5-12, 13-21.) At one point only (a section
ending at 5:4 rather than at 5:5) does he actually diverge

---

20. Stott, *Epistles*, pp. 55,56.

from the analysis above.[21] Haas, de Jonge and Swellen-grebel[22] also have simple lists of sections that have only one disagreement with my analysis although certain of my sections are put together. (The disagreement concerns a section ending at 2:29 rather than 2:28.) In the analyses of F. F. Bruce[23] and J. R. W. Stott[24] the analysis of the minor units contains no disagreement with those I have mentioned (although their analyses group the units so as to provide major sections also). Similarly the analysis of R. Brown contains only one disagreement in the analysis of minor units (ending a section at 5:4a rather than 5:5).

It seems then that there is a large measure of agreement concerning the minor units. A more difficult matter concerns whether these minor units fall into any major sections. Brown surveys 43 commentators who find major divisions in the letter. Five of them divide the letter into two (the point of division coming after 2:28 or 2:29). Thirty-four of them divide the letter into three major divisions (the points of division coming at 3:18, 3:22, 3:24, 3:24b, 4:6, 4:12 or 5:4a). Four of them divide the letter into seven major divisions.[25]

As the majority vote in the commentators surveyed by Brown would suggest, there is some reason for thinking that there are three circles in the movement of 1 John. Several matters are touched upon three times. There are three sections dealing with love (2:7-11; 3:11-18; 4:7-12), three sections which focus on obedience (2:3-6; 3:4-10;

21. Marshall, *Epistles*, pp. 22-27.
22. C. Haas, M. De Jonge & J. L. Swellengrebel, *A Translator's Handbook on the Letters of John* (UBS, 1972), pp. 14-15.
23. F. F. Bruce, *The Epistles of John*, 1970, pp. 29-32.
24. Stott, *Epistles*, pp. 55,56.
25. Brown, *Epistles*, 1982, pp. 116-130.

5:1-5), three sections which emphasize loyalty to the Johannine faith (2:18-27; 4:1-6; 5:6-12) and three passages which give reassurance (2:12-14; 3:19-24; 5:13-17).

It seems, therefore, that the structure of 1 John is best seen as three series of meditations. My proposed analysis is as follows:

1 John: **Meditations on Love and Loyalty to the Faith**

First Series of Meditations

1	*1:1-4*	The Historical Basis of the Gospel
2	*1:5-2:2*	The Basis of Fellowship
3	*2:3-6*	Obedience
4	*2:7-11*	Love
5	*2:12-14*	Reassurance
6	*2:15-17*	Not Loving the World
7	*2:18-27*	Antichrists and Loyalty to the Faith

Second Series of Meditations

1	*2:28-3:3*	Assurance at the Parousia
2	*3:4-10*	Not Sinning
3	*3:11-18*	Love
4	*3:19-24*	Reassurance
5	*4:1-6*	Testing the Spirits and Loyalty to the Faith

Third Series of Meditations

1	*4:7-12*	Love
2	*4:13-16*	God's Indwelling
3	*4:17-21*	Love Perfected
4	*5:1-5*	Faith, Love, Obedience and Overcoming the World
5	*5:6-12*	The Testimony to the Gospel
6	*5:13-17*	Knowing Eternal Life
7	*5:18-21*	Final Affirmations

1 JOHN

1: The Historical Basis of the Gospel
1 John 1:1-4

1 John 1:1-4 is concerned to emphasize the physical reality of the person of Jesus when He was in this world. Evidently some interpreters of the gospel held to a 'docetic' view of Jesus. They regarded the Christ as a phantom or spirit. John reveals his concern that the Christians have true fellowship, and the test of such fellowship is that it will be in accord with the testimony of the apostle John and his co-workers. If the apostolic testimony concerning the physical reality of the Son of God is not accepted, there will be no fellowship with the Father and the Son. In John's mind there may be true Christians whose fellowship with God has been damaged, so that they are not at this present moment in fellowship with the Father and the Son. John is not writing to his adversaries. Rather he wants his 'little children' to have fellowship with God. Such fellowship is not automatic even in the lives of true disciples.

John begins: **[1]Our theme is that which was from the beginning, which we have heard, which we have seen with our eyes, which we have beheld and our hands have handled. Our theme concerns the message of the Life. [2]And the Life was manifested and we have beheld and bear witness and announce to you that Eternal Life which was with the Father and was manifested to us. [3]That which we have seen and heard we also announce to you, in order that you also may have fellowship with us. And our fellowship is with the Father and with His Son Jesus Christ. [4]And these things we are writing to you in order that your[1] joy might be fulfilled.**

---

1. It is debateable whether the text should be 'your' or 'our'. In this kind of textual decision the flow of the argument is important. Here it requires 'your'.

The only giver of fellowship with God is the one and only Lord Jesus Christ. It is not any philosophically invented 'Jesus' who gives fellowship, nor any mythical figure who is given the title 'the Son of God'.

Who then is this Son of God?

Firstly, He was 'from the beginning'. 'Our theme is that which was from the beginning ...'. John has a habit of using deliberately ambiguous language. It has jokingly been said that 'every sentence in 1 John can be interpreted in three ways'.[2] John seems to delight in using simple words that can be taken in more than one way, and more than one way of reading them is often (but not always) valid. 'The beginning' can mean (i) before creation, (ii) the beginning of history, (iii) the beginning of Jesus' earthly ministry, or (iv) the beginning of the Christian faith of John's readers. John seems to like to leave us to choose which of his various meanings is appropriate at any particular point. Here the phrase has the first meaning because John is making the point that the *eternal* Son of God became manifested.

Secondly, this One who was from the beginning became manifested in human flesh. 'We have heard ... seen with our eyes ... beheld and our hands have handled ... the Life was manifested ... manifested to us ... we have seen and heard.' John has a repetitive style, pressing home in phrase after phrase the main points of what he wants to say. The Son of God was physically tangible. It was possible to see Him, hear Him, gaze upon Him, touch Him. It is a message embodied in a person whose being was physically real and substantial. John clearly is alluding to an

---

2 Brown, *Epistles*, p. x.

early form of the heresy of 'docetism' which regarded Jesus' body as an illusion. This meant either that Jesus did not really suffer on the cross, or that the 'Jesus' who suffered was not the same as the 'Christ, the Son of God'. The presence of the Son of God was, for such people, a masquerade. Against this, John insists that Jesus was the Son of God come in the flesh. 'Fellowship' can only come through Jesus as He really is, not through a 'Jesus' of theological imagination. Such docetism was still troublesome in the years following John and received strong opposition from Ignatius early in the second century. 'Be fully persuaded in the matter of the birth and suffering and resurrection in the time of the regime of Pontius Pilate,' wrote Ignatius, 'for these things were truly and certainly done by Jesus Christ' (*Ignatius to the Magnesians 9:1*). There were people who did not believe that the basic facts of the gospel 'truly and certainly' happened.

Thirdly, the Son of God is characterised by Life. 'Our theme concerns the message of the Life ... the Life was manifested ... we have beheld ... that Eternal Life', says John. It has always been true that 'in Him was life' (John 1:4). He *is* life (see John 11:25; 14:6). There is in Him mobility, creativeness, enabling power, holy energy, vibrant love, energetic animation, pure zeal. Other forms of life have life in Him; He has life in Himself (John 5:26). Every kind of 'life' finds its origin in God. One of the most basic descriptions of God is that He is the 'living God'. Other so-called gods are idols, the creation of human hands or human minds, gods that cannot intervene. But the essential characteristic of God is liveliness, ability to get involved with humankind, ability to speak, ability to act.

God's life was shared by the Son of God even before

He took flesh. 'In Him was life' may be said of the eternal
One who was with the Father (see also John 1:1-3). When
that 'One who was from the beginning' became flesh (John
1:14), it pleased God that the incarnate Son should have
life within Himself as the man Jesus. It is the exalted
Jesus, Son of God and truly man, who is the source and
channel of fellowship. Men and women feed on Him
because He is the bread of life (John 6:35,48). Understanding and illumination come to those who know Him as the
'light of life' (John 8:12). He dispenses 'living' water (John
4:10; 7:38) and 'living' bread (John 6:51). His words are
'spirit and life' (John 6:63) and 'utterances of eternal life'
(John 6:68). He gives life to the world (John 6:33; 10:10;
1 John 4:9).

'Eternal life' has many aspects to it. But one way of
speaking of eternal life is this: the Son of God *is* eternal
life. The Son of God has eternally been with the Father.
He is equally divine ('the true God', 5:20) yet distinct from
the Father. He has life within Himself as much as the
Father has life within Himself.

There was one generation of men who were present on
planet earth when this 'Eternal Life' was walking around
in the land of Israel. John says 'we' witnessed him. Although some want to make the 'we' to be the Christian
community (as is the case elsewhere in the letter), here
there can be no doubt that 'we' refers to the first generation of eyewitness-apostles. There is a case for arguing
that apostles are to be expected throughout human history, but there was a generation of apostles who were
unique, who were eyewitnesses of a literal incarnation and
a literal resurrection.

The apostles came into the experience of fellowship

with this Son of God, this Lord Jesus Christ. 'Fellowship' is essentially sharing the good things of God. When the apostles were with Jesus He talked to them, encouraged them, rebuked them, guided them. They on their side observed Him, picked up His ways, talked to Him, asked Him questions. For three years they shared everything with Jesus.

It was wonderful for those who were physically present with Jesus to have had fellowship with Him. But what about those in subsequent generations? John's answer is that when Christians who are not eyewitnesses of a physically manifested Eternal Life come to accept the apostolic testimony concerning Him, they begin to share the fellowship with Jesus and with the Father that the apostles have known. The apostles themselves had had to change the style of their fellowship. Jesus told them that with regard to his bodily presence He would leave them, but it would be to their advantage that He would go away (John 16:7), because when He was exalted as the king of the universe He would send them the Holy Spirit in greater measure than ever before. They would lose Him in the body but get Him back more than ever by the Holy Spirit. So John says: Believe our testimony and though you never knew Him 'according to the flesh' you will know Him as much as we apostles know Him and in the same way – by the Spirit. You will have fellowship 'with us'.

Intimate fellowship includes a distinct experience of God the Father and of His Son, our Lord Jesus Christ. We become distinctly conscious of the Father's presence and protection and provision. We become distinctly conscious of the sympathy and the heavenly intercession of the Son. It may be asked: is there a distinct fellowship with the

Spirit? To which I answer: Yes, one may be conscious of a distinct working of the Spirit pointing to the Father and the Son, but since this fellowship consists of the Spirit's pointing away from Himself to the Father and the Son, it is appropriate that the Spirit's name is not mentioned. The experience of the Spirit glorifies the Son. The Son glorifies the Father. The Spirit never glorifies Himself. For that reason He may be omitted in the account of fellowship with God.

The experience of fellowship involves fullness of joy. If knowledge of the true Jesus was real and was derived from the message of John and his fellow-apostles, it would lead to the kind of vibrant rejoicing and exultation that was characteristic of New Testament Christians. It would lead to the enthusiasm and strength of spirit that joy brings.

Yet this joy would not be simply a mystic experience of some mysterious non-physical 'Jesus'. There is no way of by-passing the testimony of the apostles to Jesus and yet still having fellowship with God. Joy will come to us only by faith in the incarnate Son of God, the Jesus of the New Testament.

Questions For Reflection: 1 John 1:1-4

1. How important is it to hold 'orthodox' views about Jesus?
2. What happens to the Christian's fellowship with God if he or she has doubts about Jesus?
3. How does fellowship lead to joy?

2. The Basis of Fellowship (part 1)
1 John 1:5-2:2

The One who gives fellowship is the incarnate Son of God (1:1-4). Now (in 1:5-2:2) John moves on to show how we can indeed have fellowship with the Father and the Son.

The section goes round the point three times, beginning in 1:5-7. There is something we need to know ('God is light ...', 1:6), and something we need to avoid ('If we say ... we are lying ...'). There is something we need to do ('But if we walk in the light ...') and something that will happen ('... we have fellowship ...').

Then John goes over the same point again, considering once more the denial that must be avoided ('If we say that we have no sin ...') and what we must do instead ('If we confess ...').

Yet a third time comes the denial to be avoided ('If we say that we have not sinned...'), and then John puts before us the very things that encourage us to walk in the light and confess our sins (2:1-2).

In 1 John 1:5-7 there is firstly *something we need to know*. **⁵And this is the message which we heard from Him and we are announcing to you. God is light and in Him there is no darkness at all**.

John and his fellow apostles heard from Jesus a message that can be summarised in this way: God is light. To 'walk in darkness' is to walk in sin. 'Light' is the opposite, it is the holiness of God, the sin-hating purity of God. 'Light' includes the revelation of God. It is the characteristic of God that He illumines; what He does in this world clarifies the human situation and makes God's will clear.

The fact that John emphasizes true knowledge and true understanding makes it sure that this too is part of what 'light' means for him.

Light is also love and joy. For John, true holiness is obedience to the love-command. It is loving every one of God's people everywhere, especially those with whom we have daily contact. It leads to fulness of joy. 'The LORD is my light' says Psalm 27:1 going on to speak of fearlessness (verse 1), strength (verse 2), confidence (verse 3), enjoyment of God (verse 4), joy (verse 6) and optimism (verse 13). Light is an expression of happiness. 'Light streams on the righteous and joy on the upright in heart' (Psalm 97:11).

This light of God is pure, undiluted, uncorrupted. 'In Him there is no darkness at all.' God will never be found tolerating sin. He cannot be content with disciples that justify sin. Clearly John's opponents are in effect saying: 'Maybe God is light, yet a little bit of darkness does not affect Him.' But 'In Him is no darkness at all!'

If we are seeking fellowship, we must remember the character of the One whose fellowship we are seeking. What would be the point of seeking fellowship with God if we have the idea that He will not mind about sinful ways?

Secondly, in these verses, there is *something we need to avoid*. If we are to enjoy fellowship with the Father and the Son, there are also things which we have to resist. Evidently the false teachers in Ephesus were in one way or another complacent about their own sinfulness. John is not writing to them, but to his own followers in Ephesus who were in danger of listening to those who had left the churches. Their teaching was apparently still influential.

Some were saying: 'One may have fellowship with God whether or not one is walking in the light in the way John says.' John says: **'If we say that we are having fellowship with Him and yet we are walking in the darkness, we are lying and we are not practising the truth.** Some Christians were evidently making the claim to fellowship but living in a way that contradicted their claim. 'We are having fellowship with God,' they said. But it was clear to John that there was much sin in their lives. The influence of the false teachers had damaged them. Clearly there was not much love in some of John's friends in Ephesus. He is not so much concerned about the false teachers who had left, for he does not say 'If *they* say ...', but 'If *we* say...'. The distinctive godliness of the Christian was missing in some of his friends. Yet they continued to claim that they were enjoying fellowship with God.

He puts it in terms of two realms: light and darkness. There is the holy realm of the character of God with its purity and its clear understanding and its joy in God, and there is the realm of darkness which is the exact opposite. One cannot be enjoying the blessing of God while one's life is characterised by the ways of godlessness. John is quite blunt in his reply. Such people are lying! The truth is something that influences our lives.

Thirdly, there is *something that we have to do*. **'But if we walk in the light as He is in the light** ... In the twentieth century East African revival the phrase 'walking in the light' was taken to mean having no secrets, making public what is happening in one's life, confessing sins publicly. This is not quite what John is saying, and sometimes the publicising of sins has been harmful. John has told us that

God is light. By 'walking in the light' he means living up
to what God shows us in His holy disclosures of His will.

These verses are not 'evangelistic' verses. John is
challenging Christian people to be in fellowship with God.
He is not querying anyone's salvation (as 2:12-14 makes
clear), but confronting his own friends with the need to be
in true fellowship with God.

It is the responsibility of Christians themselves. We have
to do something! It is something highly practical. Fellowship with God will not necessarily come simply by piety
or by plenty of praying. It is actually *walking*, a steady
step-by-step obedience in a pathway God is revealing, that
is needed.

Fourthly, if we follow John's advice, there is *something
that will happen*. Verse 7 continues: if we walk in the light
..., **we have fellowship with one another and the blood of
Jesus His Son cleanses us from all sin**. It comes as a slight
surprise that John says 'fellowship with one another'.
After 1:3 we would expect him to say 'fellowship with
God'. There is, however, a social and communal aspect to
fellowship. If we 'walk in the light', what we shall experience is not simply fellowship with God; true fellowship
with God will always involve fellowship with one another
in the Christian community.

The blood of Jesus cleanses us from sin. This is not
referring to initial salvation, but to the removal of the
obstacle to fellowship, which is consciousness of sin. It is
the cleansing of the conscience. One can be a Christian
but not (at any particular point of time) be experiencing
this. If we – we Christians – do not walk in the light, we
shall not have fellowship with God, we shall not have

fellowship with one another, and the ritual blood of Jesus will not cleanse our conscience from sin. We shall still be Christians, but our consciences will be defiled. The blood of Jesus has more than one ministry. It gives us eternal redemption and it gives us daily cleansing of conscience (see Hebrews 9:12 and 14).

The 'blood' of Jesus not only refers to the sacrifice of Jesus upon the cross, but also to the way in which that sacrifice is continuing to have a powerful influence in heaven. In the Old Testament 'blood' was viewed as the part of man which kept him alive. Similarly, the blood of Jesus keeps us alive with the things of God. 'The life is in the blood' was a basic viewpoint of Jewish thinking (see Leviticus 17:11). Westcott, the nineteenth-century commentator argued that the basic meaning of 'blood' contained 'two distinct ideas', the death of the victim and the release of the principle of life.[1] The way in which Westcott put the matter was disliked by most Bible-believing Christians because it sounded too much like the doctrine of the mass in which the death of Jesus on the cross is thought to be re-enacted, and Jesus is thought to be perpetually offering himself. Bible-believing Christians rightly rejected all of this, arguing that in Scripture the atonement of Jesus was completed on the cross.

Yet John does say that the blood of Jesus has a *present* effect. It is now, for those who walk in the light, continually cleansing from sin. This does not mean that Christ is still dying in heaven, nor that a sacrifice of Jesus is continuing in heaven. Yet there is a *present* ministry of Jesus in heaven. The matter is best understood by means of the 'Day of Atonement', the Jewish ritual in the tabernacle

1. B. F. Westcott, *The Epistles of John* (Macmillan, 1905), p. 35.

that took place at about the end of September. An animal
died for the sins of the people outside in the courtyard of
the tabernacle. Then the atoning blood was taken inside
the holy of holies, the innermost room of the tabernacle.
There it was sprinkled upon the altar. In symbol the blood
was being given to God.

Christ's sacrifice follows the same pattern. The pay-
ment of the price of sin was completed in the open courtyard of this world. Yet Jesus 'passed through the heavens'
(Heb. 4:14) and went to a place out of sight. There his
'blood' in heaven is the continuing influence of His death
applied to the believer.

There is a two-fold emphasis in the New Testament idea
of the blood of Jesus. It is not a distinction between blood-
shed-in-death and blood-releasing-life. Rather it is a distinction between blood shed in atoning sacrifice upon the
cross and blood presented to the Father in heaven. The
atoning death is finished. The continuing power of that
death continues. For those who walk in the light, despite
all remaining sinful tendencies, the blood of Jesus has
power. It goes on cleansing the believer moment-by-
moment, and the Christian has happy fellowship with the
Father and the Son.

Questions For Reflection: 1 John 1:5-2:2

1. What is it like to walk in the light?
2. How may the Christian fall into pretending to have fellowship?
3. How does the character of God affect our fellowship
with Him?

3. The Basis of Fellowship (part 2)
1 John 1:5-2:2

In his characteristically spiral way, John goes over 1:5-7 again developing a further two times what he has said (1:8-9; 1:10-2:2).

There is, firstly, *the denial that must be avoided*. The heretical teaching which has to be resisted has another aspect to it. The false teachers were evidently saying, 'We have no sin; there is no sin in us.' Over against this idea John says: **⁸If we say that we have no sin, we are deceiving ourselves and the truth is not in us**. John is alluding to some kind of dualism that held that sin resides in the material body and does not affect me, so that there is no such thing as sin in the Christian. Those who had infiltrated the churches for a while, but had then left, said that wicked behaviour did not exist in them personally. There are modern equivalents such as schools of psychology that deny guilt and responsibility, and 'new' moralities that no longer describe as sin what God describes as sin. Such teaching was influencing John's followers, just as modern Christians can be influenced by what is currently acceptable. John's friends were in danger of deceiving themselves.

Then, secondly, we find *another implication of walking in the light*. Often when God's light shines it will lead to consciousness of sin. In such a case, to 'walk in the light' means to acknowledge what we have come to see as sin. **⁹If we confess our sins, God is faithful and righteous, so that He forgives our sins and cleanses us from all unrighteousness**.

Our confession brings to light two aspects of the character of God. When we confess our sins we discover God is faithful. He does not abandon us or hold our sins against us. We discover too that God is 'righteous'. Again this word is slightly surprising. We might have expected 'faithful and merciful' rather than 'faithful and righteous'. However, forgiveness is part of God's determination to get things right, his resolution in bringing a right state of affairs into our lives.

God forgives sin, releases it, dismisses it from being taken into account. He also cleanses us from all unrighteousness. Sin leaves a stain; if there is to be a restoration of fellowship, the stain and defilement of what we have done needs also to be removed. God will see to both aspects of the matter, and we shall be able to maintain fellowship with the Father and with the Son.

Thirdly, there is *the denial to be avoided*. The issue of sinlessness was clearly a matter of dispute between John and his critics. John says: **10If we say that we have not sinned we are practising deceit and His word is not in us**. The opponents of John were saying: 'We have not actually sinned.' It seems that they were denying that sin existed at all in their followers. We have no precise knowledge of John's enemies, for John does not give them free advertising, nor does he give them the privilege of having their opinions expounded. However, we can make a good guess at the kind of thing John's opponents were teaching. Probably, in some way or other, they were claiming that their advanced 'knowledge' lifted them above the downward drag of the body so that they were characterised by sin no longer.

John has his own kind of anti-sin teaching, but it does not consist of saying that sin does not exist or does not affect our relationship to God. John, rather, insists that sin is a fact. His way of dealing with the problem of continuing sinfulness is to begin by emphasizing that it is a reality. Against the statement of his opponents John insists that continuing conflict with sinfulness is necessary. Sin continues to be an enemy to us, although this does not mean that sin is given any permission in our lives.

Fourthly, we see *what it is that encourages us in our walking in the light*. John has a way of easing the burden of guilt caused by our continuing sinfulness, but he does not want his reassurances to be misunderstood. So before he talks about God's reconciliation towards the Christian, he makes it clear that he is not giving any kind of permission to sin. **My little children**, he says, **I am writing these things to you in order that you may not sin** ... (2:1a). At this point John sounds like a perfectionist. 'You mustn't sin!' he says.

It has often been said that if we do not get *accused* of Antinomianism we have not truly preached the gospel. Yet it could be said equally: if we are not *accused* of perfectionism, we are not preaching the New Testament teaching concerning holiness.[1] In point of fact, the gospel is neither antinomian nor perfectionist – but it comes close to both!

The Christian becomes free from the burden of guilt, not by denying sin, but by means of the blood of Christ. John continues, ...**but if anyone sins we have an advocate with the Father, Jesus Christ the righteous, and He is the propitiation for our sins, and not for our sins only but also for the sins of the whole world**.

There are five encouraging aspects to John's teaching at this point.

---

1. I owe the observation to R. T. Kendall. I could add 'If we are not accused of injustice, we are not preaching the New Testament teaching concerning election' (see Romans 9:14).

It is encouraging that God is realistic about our continuing sinfulness. We do not have to pretend to be other than we are. God knows the worst about us but still accepts us. If He has accepted us without pretending that we are any different from the way we are, we can do the same. We need the blood of Jesus Christ every day. There will never come a time when we can stand in our own righteousness. There will never be a day when we can feel that we have 'arrived' at total sinlessness – until the day we see Jesus as He is.

It is encouraging to know of Jesus' advocacy on our behalf. *We have an Advocate* ...! In the heavenly throne-room where sin is weighed and judged, we have a Friend, one who argues for our forgiveness and our release.

It is encouraging to know that our Advocate is *Jesus Christ the Righteous One*. It would not do us much good if our Advocate were as sinful as we are. It would be one sinner pleading for another sinner. But our Advocate is 'Jesus', the one who was born as a baby and given the name Jesus; one who is as human as we are yet without having sinned. Our Advocate is 'Christ', the King and Sovereign who is empowered by the Spirit to achieve God's purpose of bringing us to glory. Our Advocate is 'the Righteous One', the only human being who ever deserves to be heard by God, the only one who can pray in His own name. If such a person is interceding for us, we can feel safe. He is One who always had His prayers answered on earth (John 11:42). His Advocacy will succeed now.

It is encouraging to know of Jesus' 'propitiation'. The word 'propitiation' means 'a sacrifice that turns away anger'. In His holiness God is bound to be angry with our sins. Yet since Jesus has died for us, and because His blood is being applied to our situation, the anger of God against our sin is turned aside. The idea of the 'anger' of God against sin is unfashionable, but it is found all over the Bible. No-one who believes the Bible can sensibly evade it. Would we want a God who does *not* get angry with sin? Maybe, but what we need is a Father and a Saviour-God who hates sin so much that He is determined to get rid of it, both from our own lives and from the universe around us. That is the God we have, a God who hates sin that much, a God who is angry with sin and determined to get rid of it. Maybe such a God is a fearsome Friend to have! John has a word for our encouragement: propitiation! The holy anger of God against sin has been swallowed up and removed altogether by the blood of Jesus Christ. God has nothing but friendly feelings towards us. He is satisfied with the atoning death of His own Son. We need have no fear.

It is encouraging to know Jesus' sacrifice is for every member of the human race. John adds ... *and not for our sins only but also for the sins of the whole world.* Why should John add such words? There can only be one reason: to make sure that no-one feels left out. The gnostics had a doctrine of predestination that was more extreme than anything taught by the early apostles. If the doctrine of predestination is pushed too far it is frightening. John Calvin, who was famous for his teaching on this subject, warned that if approached in the wrong way it would be terrifying; for it 'overwhelms and unsettles the conscience from its peace and tranquillity towards God'.[2] The answer to such terror is to know that Jesus died for me, and the

2. J. Calvin, *Institutes of the Christian Religion* (SCM, 1960), section 3:24:4, p. 969.

only way for me to know that Jesus died for me is for me
to know that He died for everyone. I feel safe when I know
that my sins have already been paid for. Jesus died for me.
I need never doubt that. He died for me because He died
for everyone. I need not feel left out. 'The heavenly Father
does not wish the human race that He loves to perish' (as
John Calvin put it).[3] This is a more convincing line of
interpretation than to take 'world' as meaning 'Jews and
Gentiles'. There is no discussion of 'Jews and Gentiles'
anywhere in the letter. The Jewish/Gentile relationship is
not a topic of the letter. However, assurance of God's grace
is one of the themes of the letter, and that is surely John's
point here.

Questions For Reflection: 1 John 1:5-2:2

1. How is God 'faithful and righteous' at the same time?
2. How can we fight our sinfulness without falling into
discouragement?
3. 'If we are not accused of antinomianism, we are not
preaching the gospel.' Why was Paul accused of antinomianism (Rom. 3:8; 6:1)?

---

3. J. Calvin, *The Gospel According to St. John*, 1-10 (Eerdmans, 1961),
pp. 73-74.

4. Obedience
1 John 2:3-6

Fellowship with God will result in obedience to our Lord Jesus Christ. **³And by this we know that we have known Him, if we keep His commandments. ⁴He who says 'I have known Him', and does not keep His commandments is a liar and the truth is not in him. ⁵And whoever keeps His word, in him truly the love of God is perfected. By this we know that we are in Him. ⁶He who says he remains in Him must walk in the same way that Jesus walked.**

John's point in these verses concerns a community: 'We know that we have known ...' He is not dealing with an isolated individual seeking to be sure he is truly a child of God.

His point is positive and affirming. We *do* know. It is not 'We are seeking to know whether...'. John is not inviting the kind of introspection that is full of doubts and fears concerning salvation.

The 'gnostics' were claiming revelations from God, but had no interest in Jesus' commands. John says in effect that they are a heretical cult with no knowledge of God at all. John is not concerned with discussing the reality of his readers' salvation; he has no questions about that. Instead he is concerned about what is and what is not true with regard to their 'fellowship' with the Father and with the Son.

As in 1:5-2:2, in 2:3-11 we are presented three times with the claims of the false teachers. 'He who says ... he who says ... he who says' (verses 4, 6, 9).

The change of tense in verse 3 is significant. It is not 'We know that we know...', but 'We know that we *have known* ...'. It is John's teaching that we look *back* on what claims to be from God. We reflect upon our experiences of 'fellowship' and should be able to confirm that they are from God. When John says 'Test the spirits ...' (4:1), he implies that we look *back* on what claims to have come from God. It is not something instantaneous ('We know that we know...'), but a reflection on what has happened, a looking back in time ('We know that we have known...'). 'By their fruits you shall know them,' said Jesus, but fruits take time to emerge.

Working through this passage there are eight points I want to make.

(1) *John invites us to reflect upon whether any supposed 'fellowship' with God is leading to obedience*. Sometimes we listen to a false teacher and he seems so persuasive. For a while we believe everything he says! Perhaps miracles accompany the message we are hearing. We must remember that the work of Satan can come with wonders (see 2 Thessalonians 2:9-10). But regardless of whether there is demonic help or not, it is not difficult to persuade people that miracles have taken place, even when the evidence is rather hard to find. For a while the teaching deceives even the elect, but only for a short time (see Matthew 24:24)! If the Christians follow the teaching, for a while they may be deceived into thinking they are having wonderful 'fellowship' with the Father and with the Son.

John knows that there is indeed such a thing as beautiful fellowship with the Father and with the Son, but he also knows that the false teaching in Ephesus is not of God at all. It is not having any impact in leading men and women into genuine experience of the love of God. Yet

John knows that he himself has given true teaching from God. How can he get his friends to see that his teaching is true and that of the counterfeits is false? His way is to point to the effects that the two different teachings have had. 'By this we know that we have known Him, if we keep His commandments.' The effect of fellowship with God is to lead the Christian into Jesus-like obedience. If this does not happen the teaching is suspect.

There should be nothing self-righteous about our having fellowship with God, for obedience is possible *only* because 'we have known Him'.

(2) *John warns us of the danger of deceit.* Anyone who says 'I have known Him', but does not keep the commandments that come to us through Jesus, is a liar. John puts the matter very bluntly. Such a person is a liar and the truth is not in him (2:4).

In my own ministry, I recall a time when I went to a certain conference, arranged by the theological faculty of a nearby university. Also present were two Christians I knew well. At the end of the conference one of the participants spoke at a celebration of the Lord's Supper. My two Christian friends were very impressed. 'Wasn't he wonderful!' they said. 'He was so devotional! The highlight of the conference!' Then I mentioned that I knew the writings of that theologian quite well and that in his opinion Jesus was a corpse whose bones were somewhere in Israel. He had no faith in Jesus' resurrection whatsoever and believed that all the resurrection appearances were hallucinations. In his view, 'the Lord's Supper' was nothing but looking back upon the memory of a dead friend! I knew that he had no faith in a living Saviour at all, and no personal experience of Jesus. My friends had been deceived by his 'devotional' style of talking. Sceptics can be deceptive with their 'devotional' chatter.

(3) *Truth is powerful; it has an impact upon our lives.* If 'the truth' of Jesus is working in us, it leads us powerfully into godly living. This does not mean that it works automatically. John's arguments and exhortations would not be necessary if holy living were automatic. But it means that there is a powerful pressure on us to co-operate with God. When we co-operate with that pressure and allow the truth of God to have its way, it leads into the life of love. A person may be a Christian, but if at any given point of time he is not keeping God's love-commands, at that point the truth is not 'in' him; it is not being allowed to have its effect.

(4) *God's commandments are varied forms of the love-command.* Whoever keeps His word, in him truly the love of God is perfected (2:5a). Jesus' 'Word', the entire message of the gospel, includes the love-command as its practical goal in the lives of men and women. In new birth the Word of God is planted in us (see 2:29; 3:9). We have an 'anointing' from the Holy Spirit and know that the good news about Jesus is true. As this Word works in our lives it will lead us into pathways of love. This is the love of God being 'perfected', being brought to full fruition in our lives.

(5) *Obedience to God's Word leads to fellowship.* 'By this we know that we are in Him' (2:5b). Here the phrase 'By this' probably has a general meaning: 'By this matter that I am writing about at the moment'. I have suggested that

'know that' means 'experience that'. It is obedience to the Word within us, confirmed by apostolic writings such as the one we have here in John's letter, that leads us to know in experience what it means to be 'in Him'. Obedience leads to fellowship.

(6) *John finally puts his little bit of argument into a practical command.* 'He who says he remains in Him must walk in the same way that Jesus walked' (2:6). At this point John introduces for the first time one of his favourite words: 'abide' or 'remain'. The Greek word is *meno* which simply means 'to remain, to stay in position'. It is the word used in Matthew 10:11 ('Whatever city or town you enter ... *stay* there until you go out') and Luke 1:56 ('Mary *remained* with her about three months').

In different places John speaks both of our 'abiding' and also of what 'abides' in us. He speaks of 'abiding' or 'remaining' in Jesus (2:6) or in the light (2:10) or in the fellowship of the Christians (2:19). The word is used in a slightly different way when John asks us to let the original Word of the gospel remain in us (2:24). It is when we let the Word remain in us that we are remaining in fellowship with the Father and the Son (2:24). God's anointing abides in us (2:27); we have to abide in God (2:27).

So 'abiding' has three aspects to it. (i) God's anointing given at our first conversion 'continues' or 'remains' with us. It 'abides' in us. (ii) We must let the Word of the gospel continue to work in our own lives. It must 'remain' in us by our continuing co-operation. (iii) In this way we remain in fellowship with the Father and with the Son. John will have more to say on the matter later (1 John 3:6, 9, 14, 15, 17, 24; 4:12, 13, 15, 16; 2 John 2, 9).

(7) *Faith is to be 'fulfilled' in Christian love.* John is writing to Christians whose faith is not in doubt, but he wants to persuade them to press on to show the fulness of Christian love. He wants their faith to be brought to fruition. The beginning of the Christian life is faith. The end of the Christian life is love.

(8) *A model of love is to be seen in Jesus.* We must walk in the same way that Jesus walked. The more we are in fellowship with the Father and the Son, the more that fellowship will show itself in likeness to Jesus in the way we actually live. The hidden resources of our lives will be those of Jesus. He lived by faith. He lived by the impulse of the Spirit. He lived by contact with His Father and by hearing the Father's voice. If we are in living fellowship with God, we shall be living on the same resources as Jesus.

Also, the working of the Holy Spirit will produce in us a resemblance to Jesus. Without any artificial 'imitation of Christ' we shall in fact be like Jesus, like Jesus in His great desire to please God, like Jesus in His utter self-surrender to the Father, like Jesus in laying down His life for others, like Jesus in finding His peace and His strength in the Father, like Jesus in controlling the tongue, like Jesus in His desire to do the Father's will.

Questions For Reflection: 1 John 2:3-6

1. 'Fellowship with God will result in obedience.' How is this so?
2. What is it like to 'keep God's Word'?
3. What is it like to know 'perfected love'?

5. Love
1 John 2:7-11

The greatest form of obedience is love to God and love to people. But what is love? One commentator, Raymond Brown, thought that the 'John' who wrote the letter was 'singularly unloving in dealing with those who disagreed with him', and that he might well be called the 'apostle of hatred'. The author of 1 John is like the author of John's gospel (a different person in Brown's view) in showing 'extreme prejudice'. He writes about love but does not practise it himself. His love – thinks Brown – is narrow and directed only to his own community. His words are tantamount to saying 'Love your own community and hate everyone else'![1]

Brown, however, has not understood John's heart. Love is not 'politeness'. Jesus was not being 'polite' when he denounced the Pharisees as 'whitewashed sepulchres', but there was no failure of love in Jesus.

Love is not weakness. It was not a failure of love when Jesus coolly and calmly made a whip, came back to the temple he had left and drove the small-time businessmen out of God's house of prayer. Love is not tolerance of false-hood; it is not evasiveness. A doctor who tells his patient that he has cancer is not lacking in love. The senior politi-cian in an African country who diagnosed his country as suffering from serious corruption in high places was not lacking in love. Nor is the apostle John lacking in love when he calmly but clearly repudiates the destructive her-esies of the early gnostics.

Love is not a matter of temperament. Some people are

---

1. Brown, *Epistles*, pp. x, 272.

'cholerics'; they instinctively speak in an adversarial manner. The tone of their voice is incisive. Others are
'phlegmatics'; they speak in measured tones and are seem-
ingly flat and unemotional, priding themselves on their
calmness and their lack of emotion. The 'sanguine' people are outgoing and relaxed, and may flatter themselves
that they are being more loving than others. Actually no
temperament has any advantage in the matter of love. The
'choleric' will be tempted to show his lack of love in furi-
ous bursts of indignation. He 'wears his heart on his
sleeve'. The 'sanguine' will be tempted to show his lack
of love in his own way. His eyes will be glinting and he
will speak with quiet bitterness and will give many a cool
stab in the back in what he says, despite the nice respectable manner in which he says it. Love is not a matter of
temperament at all. What is love? If we submit to the
inspired apostle, whose words are also God's Word, we
might find out.

What is 'love'? John mentions not hating brothers and
sisters, and 'laying down our lives'. He gives one example
only (3:17) and that concerns lack of compassion. He tells
us to walk just as Jesus walked (2:6; 3:3,7), but he leaves
it to us to think about how Jesus lived.

One mark of genuine Christianity is faith in the eyewitness testimony concerning the historical facts of the
gospel (1:1-4). Another test is love: how we respond when
we are ill-treated, whether we show kindness or whether
we lack kindness, our freedom from jealousy or envy, our
unfeigned graciousness towards people, our endurance
when people are difficult, our humility or lack of humility, our attitude to our 'self', our ability to control anger,
our freedom from a critical spirit, our willingness to suf-

fer for the sake of good relationships, our determination
to persist in friendship no matter what happens, our determination to make goodwill characterise everything we do.
Love can be put into words; it can be discussed.

(1) *Love is what God has always been working at.* **⁷Beloved, I am not writing to you a new commandment, but an
old commandment which you had from the beginning**. The
various commands of God are different forms of the love-
command. 'The beginning' is one of John's ambiguous
phrases and he leaves us to ponder it. Love was at the
beginning of the time we came to salvation. New converts
are often full of love. Love was there at the beginning of
the stories of particular congregations. The stories of
revivals and of new movements of the Spirit are always
characterised by great love.

Love was there at the beginning of the church. What
love the earliest Christians had for each other (most of the
time!). But the reference to Cain and Abel later in the letter
(3:12) and to the work of the devil at 'the beginning' (3:8)
shows us that John also has in mind the very earliest days
of human history. From the beginning of the human race
God has been wanting to bring about a kingdom of love.

(2) *The gospel message has at its heart a message of love.*
John says: **The old commandment is the word which you
heard** (2:7b). The preaching of Jesus was a further step in
what God had been doing since the beginning of the human
race. We are to love everyone round us, said Jesus, and pray
for enemies and persecutors (Matt. 5:43). Love, He said,
is the second part of everything the Mosaic law was demanding from Israel (Matt. 22:37-40). Love, He taught, is

the link between the Father and the Son (John 3:35; 14:31; 17:24). The love of the Father for the man Jesus was intensified because of Jesus' sacrificial love (John 10:17). God's attitude to the world is one of love (John 3:16).

Jesus' love for His disciples followed the pattern of the Father's love for them (John 15:9; 17:23). It persisted until it had completed its task on earth (John 13:1), and it was this unconditional persistent love that Jesus recommended to His disciples (John 13:34). His love was flowing through them and becoming their love (John 17:26). Their love would be seen in obedience to Jesus' commands of love (John 14:14), and would lead to rich experiences of fellowship with the Father and with the Son (John 14:21,23). This love-command was pressed upon the disciples from the very beginning (see John 15:9-17).

The love-command was there (i) in the teaching of Jesus, (ii) from the very beginning of the human race, (iii) from the very beginning of the gospel-message preached at Ephesus to John's readers.

(3) *It is also true that the love-command is ever new.* John says: **⁸Again, I am writing you a new commandment**... The command was new in that it reconstructed the rule of life. The Mosaic law had about 2,000 verses of legislation. Jesus focused God's will in one command, the command to love. If we fulfil the one principle, we shall find that we have fulfilled the entire law and the prophets (Matt. 7:12; Rom. 13:8-10). Every day we must approach the love-command as though we were hearing it for the first time in our lives. It must stay ever fresh.

(4) *The love-command is seen in Jesus.* In 2:8 John speaks of ... **a new commandment, which is true in Him** ... The new

command received a new embodiment in the person of Jesus. No-one had ever seen a human being fully obeying the love-command until Jesus walked on planet earth.

(5) *The love-command is in God's people.* Not only is it to be found in Jesus, John says it is true in Him **and also in you, because the darkness is passing away**... (2:8). Because the Christian has been rescued from darkness a new ability to love is within him.

(6) *Love is to characterise the age of world history that Jesus has brought.* John refers to the common expectation that the Messiah would bring a new and unsurpassed final epoch in the story of the human race. Before the coming of Jesus a new epoch was promised. Diagrammatically, the thinking of pre-Christian believers could be put like this.

Old Days   New Days

..../..

But then Jesus came. When he started preaching his message was 'The kingdom is at hand'. But it soon became clear that although the new days had begun, the old days had not completely finished. There was an overlap of the ages (which is perhaps the meaning of 1 Corinthians 10:11, 'upon whom the ends of the ages have come'). The position of the Christian since Jesus has come is as follows:

Old Days   New Days

..../

  /..

The new days of God's kingdom have come, but the old days of sin have not yet been entirely abolished. Yet sin is on its way out! We are to understand the present time. The old days of darkness are nearly over. The new days of the light of the kingdom of God are here already. We can start living as if we were in heaven already!

John's way of putting it is this: **a new commandment ... is true in Him and also in you, because the darkness is passing away and the true light is already shining** (2:8). We are living in the overlap! But the epoch of love has begun. Christians are living in the new days of the kingdom of love. Soon the days of darkness will be abolished altogether. We are like an immigrant moving from one country to another, but we are to concentrate on the country we are going to, not the country we have come from.

(7) *If the Christian fails in love, it is as if he has forgotten what has happened to him.* **⁹The one who says he is in the light and yet hates his brother or sister is in the darkness to this very moment**. He has been rescued from darkness, and yet he is still in darkness. He is rescued from darkness in status, in his eternal relationship to God; yet in his day-by-day behaviour he is in the dark.

(8) *We are to live in the light.* **¹⁰The one who loves his brother is remaining in the light, and there is no cause for stumbling in him**. The last phrase means that the man or woman of love will neither lead others astray nor make foolish errors himself. Love will enlighten his pathway and will keep him from foolishness.

(9) *Lack of love is confusion.* [11]**But the one who hates his brother is in the darkness and he walks in darkness and he does not know where he is going, because the darkness has blinded his eyes.** The Christian who is full of animosity is a confused person. His judgment is astray. His sense of direction is gone. His self-estimation is misguided.

Questions For Reflection: 1 John 2:7-11

1. Is John unloving?
2. How can one balance love and integrity?
3. Do different temperaments show love in different ways?

6. Reassurance
1 John 2:12-14

We can see why John should put some words of reassurance in his letter at this point. After what he has just said, some strengthening words are needed! If we were to test our fellowship by our obedience (1 John 2:3-6), especially by obedience to the love-command (2:7-11), we would no doubt conclude that we have not experienced salvation at all! Might not John's readers become introspective as the result of what John has written? He wants them to know what is and what is not true fellowship. Clearly some of John's adversaries are making a claim to fellowship which John does not want his 'little children' to receive without examination. Yet his invitation to test his adversaries' claims could lead his readers to doubt their own experience of forgiveness. This is not what John wants.

So 1 John 2:12-14 comes in at a very appropriate point in the letter. John does *not* want his readers to doubt their salvation, their past spiritual experience or their present ability to cope with the devil's assaults. He dogmatically asserts that he has no doubts at all that his readers *are* forgiven, *have* been delivered from Satan's realm, and *are* strong enough to face any foe. The fact that John is inviting his readers to test his adversaries' gospel does not mean he wishes them to fall into doubt concerning their own salvation or maturity.

Some general comments are called for at this point.

Firstly, the 'tests of conversion' approach to 1 John is refuted entirely by these verses. John is far from wanting his 'little children' to look to their personal character or their estimate of their spiritual strength in order to discover whether they are converted. Any sensitive soul who truly tries this will end up in endless introspection. It is only the Pharisee who can examine himself and then say with great assurance, 'I thank you I am not as other men', and come away with great assurance!

Secondly, for a pastor to undermine assurance of salvation never does any good. One might think that it would not do any harm if John's readers were fearful that they might not be saved; 'A little bit of terror might do them some good,' one might think! Others have thought that too much assurance of salvation was dangerous! But John does not think this way at all.

Thirdly, the New Testament motivates by love as well as by fear. The 'fear of the Lord' is not introspective doubt about salvation. It is, rather, fear of chastening, fear of displeasing God, fear of loss of reward. Assurance of salvation is one of the greatest motivators in the New Testament. A good pastor will take the trouble to keep his 'little children' rejoicing. John knows his people and specifically and emphatically gives them his assurance that he is quite certain of their salvation and of their spiritual competence.

[12]I am writing to you, little children, to tell you that your sins have been forgiven, on account of His name.

[13]I am writing, fathers, to tell you that you have known Him who is from the beginning.

I am writing to you, young people, to tell you that you have overcome the evil one.

I write to you, little children, to tell you that you have known the Father.

[14]I write to you, fathers, to tell you that you have known Him who is from the beginning.

I write to you, young people, to tell you that you are strong

and the Word of God remains in you, and you have overcome the evil one.

The style is like poetry, starting six times with 'I am writing to you ...', although the tenses differ.

John is not addressing three groups in the church; rather he is addressing two groups. 'Little children' is his term for all of his Christian friends at Ephesus (as 2:1 makes clear). Then he subdivides the entire Christian community into 'fathers' and 'young people' are his terms for the mature Christians and the young Christians respectively. The Greek may mean 'I am writing ... that ...' or 'I am writing ... because...'. The first is the likely meaning because John is strongly affirming things they need to know.

To all of his people, first, he gives a word that he is sure of their salvation. 'Your sins have been forgiven.' John wants his readers to know that they are truly Christian people. There will be no progress in the battle with the false teachers if they are not sure of their salvation. John is sure about them and he has no hesitation in letting them know how sure he is.

Forgiveness has come to them 'on account of his name'. The reason why they can feel sure about their salvation is that it does not rest at all on what they have done. It rests upon Jesus' 'name', His character and every-thing He has done for them. They can feel sure of their salvation not because they feel sure of themselves but because they feel sure about Him. Jesus is enough. If they have Jesus – and John is sure that this is the case – they have all the assurance that they need. Jesus is enough for forgiveness, enough for holiness, enough for perseverance.

Speaking next to the mature Christians, he gives them a word of encouragement. Their spiritual experience has been genuine. 'You have known Him.'

John is not referring to initial conversion (as he was in the first point). Rather he is assuring them that their experience has been genuine. The false teachers in Ephesus have not experienced God, but the true disciples of John *have* experienced God. It is not simply that they were 'converted'. John is now referring not so much to conversion but to his friends' experience of the Lord. There is such a thing as knowing God personally. God reveals Himself. He speaks and we are able to hear His voice. The more mature we are, the more we ought to know God, and know that we know Him. We are to be a people who are intensely aware of the presence of God. God is to be real to us. We are to know the joy of the Lord, assurance of salvation, boldness in speech and in action. John says, 'I am giving you my verdict about your experience. It is not the false teachers who have known God; you have known Him. Don't let anything make you doubt it.'

Then, to the young Christians he gives a word concerning their spiritual strength: 'You have overcome the evil one.' This is John's first reference to the devil. It is possible to be excessively fearful of Satan. Perhaps there were people at Ephesus telling the Christians that they were under the rule of the devil unless they submitted to everything the false teachers were telling them. John says: 'You have overcome the evil one.' The Christian overcomes Satan, in a sense, at conversion. Although it is true that the Christian can 'give place' to Satan (Eph. 4:27), yet Satan is not to be viewed as though he were as strong as Jesus. The Christian has been transferred from the kingdom of darkness to the kingdom of God's dear Son (Col. 1:13). Salvation involves new birth by the Holy Spirit; it is the dethroning of Satan in our lives. Sometimes Christians want further blessings from God but are not giving full recognition to what they already have in Jesus. We are always to be seeking more of God, but we must realise that, in a sense, the battle has already been won. '*You have overcome* ...' Defeating Satan is only a matter of working out what we already have in Jesus.

John in his typical repetitive style goes over similar ground once again in 2:13b-14.

First, he assures all his people of their genuine experience: 'You have known the Father.' He does not want them to doubt their experience of God. If they remain confident it will help their holiness, for their joy will give them confidence that they are capable of obeying Jesus' commands.

Second, he gives the same assurance again to the mature Christians: 'You have known Him who is from the beginning.' This way of putting it emphasizes that the only Jesus that John recognises is the one who is the eternal Son of God.

Third, he again assures the young people of their spiritual strength: 'You are strong and the Word of God remains in you, and you have overcome the evil one.' He has said they are strong; now he gives some added reasons. Why are they strong? Because God has implanted into their hearts His own Word. When a person is converted to Jesus Christ, the Word of God not only comes to him; it also takes root in him. From that point on he has spiritual sensitivity, because the Word of God is in him.

Both mature and young Christians need words of praise, encouragement and assurance. The next line in John's letter will be a high and holy challenge to freedom from worldliness. 'Love not the world,' he will say. But there is something the Christian needs *before* the challenge to avoid worldliness. He must know that he is in a position to face the world, the flesh and the devil. When we know we have already won the entire war, we shall defeat with ease any last little enemies that come our way. The joy of the Lord will be our strength, rather than the misery of doubt being our weakness. John knows this and, as a skilful pastor, gives the word of encouragement before he gives the high challenge. Some might say, 'I do not feel strong. I think the devil is defeating me.' John replies, 'You have all the grace you need because Jesus is with you.' R. T. Kendall quotes a poem:

> Oh what joy we often forfeit,
> Oh what victories we lose,
> Oh what power we never feel,
> All because of grace we did not use.[1]

Questions For Reflection: 1 John 2:12-14

1. Why does John affirm his readers' salvation at this point?
2. How important is assurance of salvation?
3. How should we give assurance of salvation to others?

---

1. Kendall, *Affirming the Grace We Already Have*, WR, Feb 1984, p. 8.

7. Refusing to Love the World
1 John 2:15-17

After the rich words of encouragement in the previous passage, John mentions the danger of what is normally called 'worldliness'. He directs attention not to breach of law-codes but to inward appetites and to pride; matters that receive minimal attention in 'the law' of Exodus-Leviticus-Numbers-Deuteronomy.

First comes a command **¹⁵Do not love the world nor the things in the world**. 'The world' is not the fabric of the universe. Nor is he simply talking about earthly blessings or the structures of society. It is not 'worldly' to follow a career in politics, to get married, to have children, to be involved in earning a living. None of these are what John has in mind by 'the world'.

Nor is John concerned about a list of 'taboos'. Every group of Christians has a list of activities or practices that are frowned upon. Christians tended to think, in days gone by, that 'worldliness' was a matter of whether one went to dances or to the cinema. Such 'taboos' vary from age to age. What was forbidden ten years ago is allowed today. Such banned activities also vary from culture to culture. In one part of the world Christians might frown upon bare arms, or upon earrings, or on allowing the soles of the feet to become visible ... or whatever! But none of this is what John has in mind.

The word 'world' has various meanings. Here it is a disposition, an outlook, a frame of mind. It is the anti-God mentality of the human race, the worldwide fondness for sin and self which causes men and women to stumble into wickedness. 'Woe to the world because of occasions of stumbling,' said Jesus (Matt. 18:7). It is rebelliousness, spiritual ignorance (1 John 3:1; John 1:10), combined with hostility towards God (see James 4:4). Behind it is the grip of Satan (see 1 John 5:19). 'Worldliness' is the inclination to be drawn into the ways of the people around us who do not know God.

'The things of the world' are the ways in which the world's magnetism operates. To refuse to love the world means a decisive rejection of the 'world's' aspirations and outlooks. It is not going out of earthly society altogether, but it is a refusal to be dragged into its grumbling, its bitterness, its covetousness, its obsession with 'cares and riches and pleasures' (Luke 8:14), its preoccupation with receiving praise from fellow human beings.

Secondly, John has two reasons why we should not love the world. One is that 'worldliness' excludes God's love (2:15b-16) and the other is that the world is doomed to be destroyed and only love for God will survive (2:17).

Love of the world will drive out love for God. **If anyone loves the world, the love of God is not in him** (2:15b). 'Love of God' is an ambiguous phrase. Is it 'love for God' (this is probably the main thought), or is it God's love for us, or is it divine love, the love for people that comes into our lives because God is at work? John leaves us to take it how we will. A glance at the eight times this phraseology is used will show us that the phrasing seems to be equally ambiguous in John 5:42 and 1 John 2:5. But in John 15:10 and 1 John 4:9 the first meaning seems predominant; in 1 John 3:17 and 1 John 4:12 the third meaning seems predominant; and in 1 John 5:3 the second meaning would fit

best. In this verse John's words are true whichever of these
ways we take! Loving the world is a failure to love God; it
is failure to grasp hold of how much God loves us; it is
bound to show itself in failure to truly love other people.

Next comes a statement of the three channels along which
the world attacks us: **¹⁶For all that is in the world, the desire
of the flesh and the desire of the eyes and the pride of life, is
not from the Father but is from the world.** John describes
how there are three routes along which we are pulled into
worldly ways. 'The desire of the flesh' is the pull into wickedness that comes to us through our physical appetites,
our sexuality, our physical tiredness and moodiness, our
desire to protect ourselves, our hunger and thirst. 'The
desire of the eyes' is the way in which sin's pull is intensified when we see something that attracts us. 'I saw ... then
I coveted' said Achan (Josh. 7:21). Potiphar's wife 'lifted
up her eyes towards Joseph' and wanted to sin (Gen. 39:7).
The 'pride of life' is the tendency we have to exalt ourselves, to manipulate ourselves to look good in the eyes of
others, to grasp after admiration.
    From at least the fifth century it has been noted that all
three of these channels of temptation were operating in
the temptation of Jesus. The tempter came at a time when
Jesus was hungry and appealed to his physical appetite
('command that these stones become bread'). He appealed
to the 'desire of the eyes' when he *showed* Him all 'the
kingdoms of the world'. And he appealed to Jesus' desire
for glory when he offered Jesus the prestige of ruling the
kingdoms of the world (Matt. 4:1-11; Luke 4:1-12). The
same three channels of temptation were operating in the
story of Adam and Eve (Gen. 3:1-6). The woman saw that

the tree was good for food (the 'desire of the flesh') and was a delight to the eyes (the 'desire of the eyes') and that it was desirable to make one wise (the 'pride of life').

Such enticements to sin do not come from the Father but from 'the world'. No-one can serve two masters. Love of the world will exclude love of the Father; or love of the Father will exclude love of the world. Remember that in all of this John is addressing Christians. He has just given them great assurance. 'Your sins have been forgiven ... you have known Him ...you have overcome ... you are strong and the Word of God remains in you ...'. He is not speaking evangelistically to people whose salvation he regards as dubious. This ought to let us know that sanctification is not automatic and needs great attention on the part of preachers and pastors. It ought also to keep us from undermining assurance of salvation ('If you could do a thing like that I do not think you are truly converted!'). And it ought to give us great encouragement. John assures us that if we trust in Jesus our salvation is sure, and we are able to accept the invitation to break free from love of the world by finding strength in love of the Father. It is all immensely liberating.

John goes on to speak of the reward for staying free from worldliness and keeping in the love of God. World-liness does damage to us, but there is a reward for doing the will of God. He adds: **[17]And the world is passing away with its desires, but the person who does the will of God remains for ever.**

The penalty for love of the world is some kind of nullifying of our works that have displeased God, and the obliteration of that aspect of our lives as useless. It is often said in Scripture that the wicked be nothing but ashes, that they will vanish like smoke, that even their memory will perish. The works of sin have no permanence. Every part of our lives that is dominated by love for the world is doomed to be useless and to be destroyed. "The world is passing away with its desires".

It is what has been done out of love for God that will continue. The reward for loving God is 'abiding', 'remaining', 'continuing'. Everything that arises out of the love of God has eternal value and in some way will survive. (In 1 Corinthians 3:14 Paul speaks of what happens 'if any person's work shall remain' amidst the fires of God's judgment.) Permanence is part of the reward. What is done out of love for God is 'laying up treasure in heaven'. 'The person who does the will of God remains for ever.'

John does not use the word 'law' (despite some translations of 1 John 3:4), but he speaks rather of doing 'the will of God'. The term is very comprehensive. There are many things involved in 'the will of God' that may not be included in the word 'law'.

One thinks of the many times in the Bible where someone seeks the will of God but no answer could possibly have come by any kind of legislation. David might seek to know whether he should attack a city (see 2 Sam. 2:1), or how he should express his indignation at the murder of Saul's relatives (see 2 Sam. 4:5-12), or how to capture Jerusalem (see 2 Sam. 5:6-7). The law gave no help in these situations, yet in each of them there was 'the will of God'. The early church might fast and pray for guidance for its next step forward. But when 'the will of God' came to them it was not in the form of legislation (see Acts 13:1-2).

The 'will of God' is a larger and broader concept than the Mosaic law. It is everything that God makes known to us by the Word and by the Spirit as being His will for our lives. Every person who does the will of God will remain for ever and his works will remain for ever. The 'Well done' of Jesus will last eternally.

Questions For Reflection: 1 John 2:15-17

1. What is worldliness?
2. How can one be free from worldliness without legalism?
3. What consequences does worldliness have in our own lives?

8. Antichrists and Loyalty to Faith (part 1)
1 John 2:18-27

John's concern is with a heretical group of imitation-Christians in and around Ephesus. His letter is highly practical. It is concerned not with pure theology but with the impact false teaching is having in the lives of his 'little children'. He is not hesitant to speak plainly. Teaching that does not lead to godliness is a lie! Teaching that denies that Jesus is the Son of God in the flesh is a lie! There is no way that there can be fellowship with God among those who will not confess that the man Jesus is the divine Christ.

Now John relates all of this to predictions concerning Antichrist.

First, he reminds them of the predictions they had heard. **¹⁸Little children, it is the last hour; and as you heard that Antichrist is coming, so now many antichrists have arisen. From this we know that it is indeed the last hour**. The term 'last hour', like the expressions 'last days' (Acts 2:17; 2 Tim. 3:1; Heb. 1:2; 2 Peter 3:3) and 'last times' (1 Peter 1:20; Jude 18), refers to the period between the first coming and the second coming of Jesus. It began with the coming of Jesus. Hebrews 1:2 speaks of '*these* last days'. The coming of Jesus inaugurated the kingdom of God and introduced the last epoch of human history. It will be brought to consummation when Jesus comes the second time, but the 'last days' have already begun.

Jesus had foretold that before the fall of Jerusalem false prophets would come (Matt. 24:11), but this would *not* introduce the end of the world (Matt. 24:6); they would be only the *beginning* of sufferings (Matt. 24:8). Paul, writ-

74

ing to Timothy in Roman Asia (the same locality in which John was now ministering), had also warned of perilous times (2 Tim. 3:1-9).

In John's day it was apparently well-known among John's friends that it was the last epoch of the human race (as it still is) and that 'Antichrist' was on his way. The prophecies of Daniel had spoken of a powerful enemy of God rising to persecute God's people (Dan. 7:8, 24-25). The prediction was partly fulfilled in the second century BC in the person of Antiochus Epiphanes, but it was expected that there would be further figures in the history of the world who would be like Antiochus. Jesus predicted that the time of the fall of Jerusalem would be a time when an 'abomination of desolation' would ruin the temple of Jerusalem. In AD 70 Roman soldiers set up their pagan symbols in the temple court while the sanctuary was being burnt. Paul predicted a 'man of sin' some time in the history of the church (2 Thess. 2:3-4). Similar predictions come in the book of Revelation (11:7; 13:1-18; 17:3-17; 19:19-20).

John uses the term 'Antichrist'. The word has virtually become a name and should be given a capital letter. John urges that there may be little 'antichrists', advance previews of the final figure. When false teachers were troubling the churches, they were little 'antichrists'. It was precisely what was to be expected and was an indication that they were indeed in 'the last days' (2:18).

Next, John wants his friends to see how the intruders related to the churches in which he ministered (2:19-21). The false teachers had apparently attached themselves to churches, but they had never been authentically Christian.

While they were among the Christians they sought to act
as though there were no differences between John's
teaching and their own. John says **19They went out from us,
but they were not of us. For if they had been from us, they
would have remained with us, but they went out in order
that it might be made clear that none of them were of us.**
They had hoped to find ready-made congregations to take
over and use to propagate their own teaching. The Christians had never totally yielded to their influence, and after
a while the false teachers realised they could not achieve
their aims and they abandoned their efforts and left the
Johannine churches.

The intruders had never been converted to Jesus Christ.
They had no Christian experience arising out of the testimony of the Christian church. In this sense, says John,
'they were not from us'. God uses His people to bring
fresh additions to His church. Christians are 'of' the church
in the sense that conversion to Jesus Christ arises from the
proclamation and witness of God's people. But the false
teacher with his false gospel 'does not enter the sheepfold
by the door'. He gets into the company of the church of
Jesus 'by another way' (John 10:1), and his ministry is
not authentic. He is a 'thief and a robber' (John 10:2).

As time went on, the difference between the intruders
and the Christians became clear. Their proselytizing failed
and they left the churches. Their breakaway made it clear
that they never had been part of the church of Jesus Christ.

Today, regarding the parts of 'the church' which deny
that Jesus is the Son of God come in the flesh, John's reaction would have been the same. Some sections of 'the
church' today he would not regard as authentically Christian. He would have used any authority he had to protest

that a 'Jesus' who was not the incarnate Son of God
neither existed nor could be a Saviour. Modern day false
teachers would have been excluded by him. He would have
insisted that the religion of those who deny the Jesus of
the Bible ought not to be called 'Christianity'. He would
not have regarded lightly a situation where the believers
in the gospel were a 'party' or 'wing' of the church. He
would have made it lucidly clear that the reality of Jesus
Christ as the Son of God in the flesh is essential to the
gospel. He undoubtedly would have called some ministers of the church today 'antichrists'.

John's spiritual children had not been deceived for very
long. John says **[20]But you** – the Greek for 'you' is emphatic – **have an anointing from the Holy One, and you all
have knowledge**.

In the New Testament teaching there are three levels of
receiving the Spirit. (i) The Spirit works in our hearts below the level of consciousness to work faith in our hearts
and to give new birth (1 Cor. 2:14; 12:3; see comments
below on 1 John 5:1). (ii) The Spirit is given at a higher
level to seal sonship in those who have been brought to
faith (Eph. 1:13, 14; Gal. 4:6). (iii) The Spirit is given at a
yet higher level in the resurrection body (1 Cor. 15:44
where 'spiritual' refers to the Holy Spirit). The word
'anoint' is used in connection with all three levels of receiving the Spirit.

Here in 1 John 2:20, 27 'anointing' refers to what Calvin
called 'the secret work of the Spirit' in bringing people to
faith and new birth. Elsewhere 'anointing' is used with
reference to the Spirit's giving assurance and a foretaste
of glory (2 Cor. 1:21, 22; 5:5). In one place the word
'anoint' is used of the occasion when Jesus was raised to a

level of glory above his companions, the angels (Heb. 1:9).[1]

In 1 John 2:20, 27 the reference is undoubtedly to what happens as the Holy Spirit brings the individual to faith. The anointing comes from Jesus, 'the Holy One'. It is given to every Christian. No-one becomes a Christian without the anointing of the Spirit. The Spirit gives illumination and enables a grasp of the truth. By nature everyone is blind to spiritual things. No-one by nature receives the things of God as trustworthy. No-one by nature can call Jesus 'Lord'. No-one, by nature, can please God or submit to the God of the Bible.

It is the initial anointing of the Holy Spirit that changes all this. The Holy Spirit causes 'light to shine out of darkness' (2 Cor. 4:6). False teachers may throw the Christian off balance for a while, but the false teacher cannot persuade the Christian to adopt a heretical 'gospel'. Every Christian *at that point* has an anointing and *knows* that there is something false when he is confronted with destructive heresies with regard to the person of Christ. False teachers do damage for a while, but the elect cannot be deceived, at this point. The church of Jesus continues and the gates of hell do not prevail against it.

John says **[21]I have not written to you because you do not know the truth, but on the contrary because you do know it, and because no lie is of the truth**. John's friends have already come to the conclusion that these teachers of Ephe-

---

1. This way of putting the matter is unusual, but George Smeaton (whose orthodoxy cannot be doubted) speaks of three 'grades' or 'degrees' in which the Spirit was experienced by Jesus. His points correspond exactly to mine (see G. Smeaton, *The Doctrine of the Holy Spirit*, Banner of Truth, 1974, pp. 128-149). He quotes in connection with Jesus (i) Luke 1:35; 2:40; (ii) John 1:33; Acts 10:38; (iii) Acts 2:33.

sus are heretical. John is writing simply to confirm the conclusion they have already reached, and also to keep them firm lest they should be damaged by the continuing influence of the false teachers.

Why does John have to assure them that they know the truth? It is because they have been tempted to listen to the false teachers. They had listened and were feeling bad that they had done so. However, they have never been fully persuaded that the gnostics were right, for the anointing of the Holy Spirit kept them from accepting everything the gnostics had said. So what now? Do they need to discover the truth all over again? John says to them: 'I am not writing something new to you. You already know enough of the gospel to recover. You do know the truth. Simply come back to it wholeheartedly. Realise that this is a black-and-white matter. The gnostics are believing a lie. Any teaching which denies the Son of God is come in the flesh is a lie. Trust in the anointing which you already have. I have complete confidence in you' – says John – 'because I know that you received the gospel. I know that the anointing is still with you at this very moment. Recognize that gnosticism has no relation to the truth at all. Depend on Jesus, the one-and-only Son of God in human flesh, and you will be instantly restored.'

Questions For Reflection: 1 John 2:18-27

1. If the 'last days' have lasted so long, should we be expecting Jesus to come soon? Really?
2. Can there be little 'antichrists' before the big Antichrist?
3. Will the church always defeat heresy?

9. Antichrists and Loyalty to Faith (part 2)
1 John 2:18-27

John has spoken of the predictions concerning false teachers (2:18), and he has explained what has recently happened in the churches (2:19-21).

Now John pinpoints the false teaching that was involved. **²²Who is the liar but the one who denies that Jesus is the Christ?** He uses the definite article ('*the* liar'; the Authorised Version is mistaken). Some have thought this is an allusion to Cerinthus, the docetic heretic. There is a story that John once went to the public baths at Ephesus, found that Cerinthus was there, and left hastily saying, 'Let us flee, lest the baths fall in while Cerinthus, the enemy of the truth, is within.'[1] On the other hand, Cerinthus is not mentioned by name in 1 John, and some teachings of Cerinthus get no mention in 1 John. Also, there is a connection between the heretics mentioned in 1 John and the false teachers living in the Roman province of Asia who are mentioned in the writings of Ignatius. However, again there seem to be differences.

It is best to interpret 1 John wholly within its own terms of reference and use our knowledge of Cerinthus and the writings of Ignatius only to illustrate the heresies mentioned. The situations are similar, but John chose not to spell out in detail the way the heretics put their teaching. We must be content to know the small amount that we can deduce from his letter. The article ('the') in verse 22 is probably used to pinpoint the fact that to deny the identity

---

1. Irenaeus, *Against Heresies* 3:3:4. The story is said to go back to Polycarp, who apparently knew the apostle John personally.

of Jesus as the Son of God come in the flesh is *the* great heresy, the arch-lie.

The essence of the false teaching was the denial that Jesus is the Christ. 'Christ' in 1 John includes the idea of Jesus' being the divine Son of God. Acknowledging the Christ and acknowledging the Son of God (4:15) are parallel expressions. The false teachers acknowledged there was such a person as Jesus, and they believed there was such a being as the divine 'Christ', but they did not want to identify Jesus as the divine Christ. It was a heresy that resembles that of some modern theologians who do not wish Jesus to be described as 'God'. John teaches (notably in John 1:14) that the divine pre-existent Son of God became 'flesh', that is to say, became a particular human being with a genuine human nature. In 1 John he teaches that Jesus is the Christ (2:22) or the Son (2:22-23). He says that Jesus Christ has come in the flesh (1 John 4:2; 2 John 7).

From what we know of false teaching in Roman Asia Minor the heretics would have believed that some kind of divine power, a 'spiritual' (non-material) 'Son of God' came down upon the man Jesus at his baptism and left him before the crucifixion (a teaching referred to in 1 John 5:6). They denied that the man Jesus was to be identified totally with the Son of God. And they denied that the Son of God died upon the cross. (Islam also has traditions in it that go back to these early heresies. According to the *Qur'an* Jesus did not die on the cross, but was taken to heaven, leaving someone else to be crucified in his place. Again the idea is that a man such as Jesus could not truly have died such a death.)

John mentions lying. One might think he would actu-

ally quote Exodus 20:16, but John has higher concerns
than what is mentioned in the ninth commandment. For
John, at this point, 'lying' is to be defined not legally but
Christologically. The sin is not a perjury in a law-court,
bearing false testimony before the judges, but a lie against
the person of Christ. John defines sin with reference to
Jesus more than with reference to the ten commandments.

It is not possible to hold false teaching in this matter
and have fellowship with God. **²³Anyone who denies the
Son does not have the Father either. The person confessing
the Son also has the Father**. People who deny the deity of
Jesus may think that they have the blessing of God. But
the 'god' they believe in is an idol. The one-and-only-God
is the 'God and Father of our Lord Jesus Christ'. To fail to
receive Jesus as the Son of God in the flesh is to lose the
Father's presence. It is to lose His protection, His promises and His provision, and finally to forfeit heavenly glory
and thus to lose His paradise.

A word of advice follows: **²⁴As for you, let what you
heard from the beginning remain in you. If what you heard
from the beginning remains in you, then you will remain in
the Son and in the Father**. The Christian's position 'in
Christ' is the source for everything he needs. He will need
to seek more and more of God, but his position is right.
He only has to 'continue' feeding on Christ. From 'the
beginning' he has been entering into the wealth of what is
there for him in Jesus. The Christians heard a message.
Faith comes by some kind of 'hearing'. John asked them
not to move from what they heard at first. They are to
explore its depths and riches but they cannot improve their
basic position. They need no change in their view of the
person of Jesus. The gnostics wanted them to modify their

understanding of and their dependence on Jesus as the Son of God. John says to them, 'Continue to depend on the Jesus you discovered when you first heard the gospel. If you do that, you will be having fellowship with the Son of God and fellowship with the Father himself.'

If they remain in position they will experience the blessings of God. They will know the Son, they will know the Father. **²⁵And this is the promise which He promised us, eternal life**. 'Eternal life' does not refer here to initial conversion. John is not urging them to become Christians, nor is he urging them to be sure to get to heaven. 'Eternal life' often (as here) refers to the day-to-day experience of the vitality of God. Paul said to Timothy: 'Lay hold of eternal life' (1 Tim. 6:12). 'Eternal life' is the daily experience of entering into a life that comes from God. It is the working of the Holy Spirit 'springing up' (John 4:14) within us. It is liveliness daily experienced by heeding the words of Jesus (John 6:68). The life of God burns within us. Eternal life is being lively people with the liveliness that comes not from temperament or physical health but from God. It is promised to us and it will come to us in experience if we are leaning on the same Jesus who saved us at 'the beginning'.

In the last lines of this unit (2:26-27), John again urges that the anointing they have received is adequate for them. If they trust the Holy Spirit all will be well. **²⁶I write these things to you concerning those who would deceive you**. Destructive imitations of the gospel and rivals to the Christian gospel can be very attractive and alluring. Like a seductress, a reduced or perverted gospel comes with a smiling face and attractive poise. But to heed the gnostic gospels – ancient or modern – will result in shame, fear, loss of spiritual power and loss of fellowship.

They are told the anointing will remain in them. **²⁷And as for you, the anointing which you received remains in you and you do not have any need that anyone should teach you. On the contrary, as His anointing teaches about all these things, and as that anointing is true and is not a lie, and as He has taught you – remain in Him**. They will not lose the anointing, but they are also told to make use of what they have. 'The anointing remains ... you remain also!' There is a promise of God's continued illumination, yet if they are to have the full experience of eternal life on a day-by-day basis they must boldly and confidently remain where God first put them. They have a promise of *continued* anointing and *trustworthy* anointing, so on their side they must again trust and boldly confess their faith in Jesus, the Son of God come in the flesh. Then they will experience the life of God welling up within them again.

They also now have the added stability of having the matter put into writing by the inspired apostle. The Holy Spirit leads us into the truth. It was the Holy Spirit who led the first generation of Christians into the truth concerning Jesus. Yet the New Testament comes into the matter as well. John was an inspired, first-generation apostle, a literal eyewitness of the incarnation and the resurrection. He is putting his teaching into writing, and his letter has become part of our New Testament. The Holy Spirit does the teaching, but the witness of first-generation inspired men came in to confirm the teaching and give a double confirmation as to what is and what is not the gospel. 'The things I have written ... the anointing ... remains' point to the written Word and the illuminating Holy Spirit. The Holy Spirit ought to be enough, but there will be instability in the churches unless the written Word comes in also.

John has not written because they do not know the truth; they know it already by the Holy Spirit, but all sorts of people make weird claims to the Holy Spirit, so there needs to be some extra witnesses. John appeals to the witness of history (1:1-4) and to his own position as a first-generation apostle bearing witness to that history.

So he explains what he is doing. They are strong but have been through an attack of the devil in the form of these false teachers who have tried to deceive the churches (2:26). But the Holy Spirit will be adequate for them to stand firm. They only have to remain in Jesus, the incarnate Son of God (2:27).

Questions For Reflection: 1 John 2:18-27

1. How can one be courteous but firm with those who deny Jesus' deity?
2. How human was Jesus? Did He get depressed? Could He have wanted to get married?
3. Does it matter that Jesus is God and man at the same time?

10. Assurance at the Parousia
1 John 2:28-3:3

In 1 John 2:28 John starts his second circuit round the 'spiral staircase' of his meditations and begins to refer to some of his topics for the second time. 'Abiding' is now related to Jesus' second coming.

(1) First, John *calls his people to 'remain' in Jesus*: **²⁸And now, little children, remain in Him, in order that if He is manifested we may have confidence and may not be ashamed so as to shrink from Him in His coming.** One day Jesus will come a second time, suddenly, unexpectedly, literally, visibly, personally, gloriously, triumphantly. His coming is called being 'manifested' because at present Jesus is physically not able to be seen. His coming is also called His 'arrival' (the Greek word is *parousia*).

(2) After this call to remain in Jesus, John feels it is right *to provide a criterion concerning the protection of fellowship*: **²⁹If you know that He is righteous, you know that it is also a fact that everyone who does righteousness has been born of Him.** Verse 28 leads to verse 29 in the following way: 'Abiding' in Jesus involves having 'fellowship with one another', but who exactly is included in the 'one another'? Only those who share in the righteousness of the character of God. John's people need fellowship, but it will do them no good having any supposed fellowship with the gnostics of Ephesus. The starting point for being ready for the Coming of Jesus is new birth.

John is not saying, 'Only if you can be sure you are practising righteousness can you be sure of your salvation.' Rather, the readers have here an invitation to discern who is and who is not an authentic bearer of the word of Jesus. They are invited to judge not themselves but the teachers of a false interpretation of the gospel. If they know that Jesus is the Righteous One – as they do – then they should *also* know that, among the differing religious movements in the Ephesus area, those who practise righteousness (in accordance with the very nature and title of Jesus) are the ones born of Him. It is notable that John uses the third person here. He does not say, 'If you know that He is righteous, then you know that if *you* do what is right *you* have been born of Him.' The third person pronouns indicate that it is assessment of movements in the Ephesian community that is at stake. They do know that Jesus is the Righteous One; they ought to evaluate the claims of the proto-gnostic movement accordingly. The logic of the sentence is: 'If you know about *Jesus*, you know about *them*.'

What is involved in 'doing righteousness'? In John's thinking it involves confessing that Jesus is the Son of God come in human flesh, submitting to the message that has come through the apostolic witnesses of the resurrection, and living a life of love towards the Christian brotherhood. Only such people are 'born of God'. If the Christians at Ephesus are to remain in Jesus (2:28), they will have to have fellowship with those who 'do righteousness' in this way, and they will have to know who they are.

John mentions the new birth for the first time in 1 John 2:29. It will be mentioned more than once from this point onwards (see 3:9; 4:7; 5:1,4,18; see also John 1:13; 3:6,8).

(3) Next comes *an invitation to consider the present privileges of being God's sons* (3:1). John has his mind set on the 'Parousia', the occasion when the Christian's sonship receives its greatest climax. But John does not want anyone to think that the Christian's sonship begins for the first time at the Parousia, so he deals with present sonship first. The prospect of the Parousia (2:28) and the Christians' refusal to be misled by the proto-gnostics (2:29) should lead them on to preparing for the Parousia. But first they start by considering the present stage of their sonship. **¹See what love the Father has given us that we should be called children of God; and that is what we are! The reason why the world does not know us is that it did not know Him.**

Although the greatness of God's love is seen in their present sonship (3:1a), unrecognized by the world (3:1b), yet there is a further stage in sonship to be revealed at the Parousia (3:2). When this hope is grasped it leads to self-purifying (3:3).

John's thought in verse 1, then, is that although sonship is a great privilege and the greatest way in which God has shown love, yet the Christians must expect their sonship to go unrecognised by the world.

(4) Next is *a call to be ready for the revelation that will take place when Jesus comes* (3:2). Verse 1 was a preliminary to verse 2. The Christian's sonship will not be hidden for ever. **²Beloved, we are God's children now, and it does not yet get manifested what we shall be. We know that if He is manifested we shall be like Him, because we shall see Him as He is.** At the Parousia the sonship of the Christian will be heightened and made visible. There is a final blessing of being God's children: we shall be redeemed from the pres-

ence of sin. The consequences of sin will be obliterated. We shall have a body that radiates with the brightness of holiness, that is imperishable, unable to deteriorate and honourable, a body of dignity and excellence, conformed to the glory of our Lord Jesus Christ. The sight of Jesus will transform us.

(5) Lastly in this unit comes *a practical point, drawn from what he has said in 2:28-3:2.* When the hope of the Parousia is grasped, it will lead to our purifying ourselves from sin. The underlying thought is that our becoming like Jesus at the last day is in fact our present-day godliness becoming visible. If our level of righteousness will one day become visible, we are spurred on to cleanse ourselves from unrighteousness and to follow the love-commands of Jesus. **³And everyone who holds this hope in Him purifies himself, just as He is pure.**

It is widely thought that John is teaching the inevitable and irresistible self-purification of all Christians. 'If heaven is the destination, we must be travelling the road that leads there,' says David Jackman. He adds 'Notice how carefully John rules out any exception. This applies to every Christian'.[1] P. Bonnard emphasizes that this self-purification must be consciously taken up by the believer; 'It does not come automatically.' Yet he also sees this verse referring to 'All believers ... not a particular category of believers'.[2] Despite what Jackman and others say, John most certainly is referring to some (and not all) believers when he speaks of 'Those who hold to this hope ...'. If the argument is followed carefully this becomes clear. He has

---

1. D. Jackman, *Message of John's Letters*, 1988, p. 85.
2. P. Bonnard, *Les Epitres Johanniques*, 1983, p. 68 (my translation).

already given his readers an assurance of their salvation
(2:12-14), yet he goes on to urge them to remain in Jesus
so as not to shrink back in shame when Jesus comes. Evidently John teaches that some believers *will* shrink back
in shame at Jesus' coming. He is not addressing the world
or his enemies in Ephesus. He speaks of 'our' not shrinking
in shame, and evidently thinks it will happen to some. We are
to remain in Jesus so that this does not happen. For those
who do not remain in Jesus it *will* happen. When John
speaks of 'he who holds this hope ...' he is not referring to
all Christians, but to those Christians who remain in Jesus.

Much depends on how 'having this hope on him' is
interpreted. John refers to *having* (*echo*) this hope, and
the Greek word *echo* is a stronger word than 'have' is in
English. There are several places in the New Testament
where writers refer to 'holding' a hope and where the
reference is a firm and sure grasp. When Paul speaks in
2 Corinthians 10:5 of 'holding (*echontes*) the hope that ...
our field may be ... enlarged', he is referring to grasping
hold of what is possible for his ministry in the future.
Elpida ... echontes (holding ... hope) is a stronger expression than *elpizontes* (hoping). When in Acts 24:15 we read
of Paul's 'holding (*echo*) a hope towards God which these
men themselves also cherish (*prosdechomai*)', it is clear
that 'holding' a hope and 'cherishing' a hope are the same,
and the meaning of *echo* in this context approximates to
that of *prosdechomai*, 'to take up, welcome, cherish'. When
Ephesians 2:12 says Gentiles were 'not holding to any
hope' (*elpida me echontes*), the surrounding context in
Ephesians chapter two is dealing not merely with objec-
tive position but with subjective state. The Gentiles were
not grasping hold of the hope of Israel. In 1 Thessalonians

4:13 'not holding to any hope' (*me echontes elpida*) is explicitly synonymous to 'grieving' (as *lupesthe* indicates).

One notices occasions where the New Testament explicitly refers to 'holding to one's hope', but uses a less ambiguous verb than *echo*. Hebrews 3:6b speaks of a privilege that comes to the believer 'if we hold (*kataschomen*) exultation in our hope'. Hebrews 6:18 says we have 'the hope set before us' and that we must 'lay hold (*kratesai*)' of it. All of this suggests that 1 John 3:3 is not referring to what irresistibly and inevitably happens to each Christian. It is not the case that every Christian 'purifies himself just as Jesus is pure'. Rather John's point is that the Christian who 'holds' this hope will purify himself. There is the possibility for the Christian that he will not hold this hope; such a Christian becomes careless. When Jesus comes he will shrink back in shame. His salvation is not suspect, but at the Parousia he faces dishonour.

Certainly John is urging godly living here, yet he is not undermining the Christian's salvation. He regards the Christian task of self-purification as sufficiently voluntary as to require exhortation and argument to bring it about in his disciples. He does not give a hint as to the possibility of their not being Christians. At the same time he urges that further progress must be made in their lives if they are not to be ashamed at the Parousia.

Questions For Reflection: 1 John 2:28-3:3

1. Do you think it possible for you to be confident in the day of Jesus' coming?
2. Does every true Christian cleanse himself from sin?
3. What does it mean to 'remain' in Jesus?

11. Not Sinning (part 1)
1 John 3:4-10

A Christian speaking of her student days could say of 1 John 3: 'I feared this chapter with a strange kind of horror ... I was frightened of indulging in spiritual dishonesty, of accepting explanations just because they suited me, suited what I wanted to believe.'[1] 1 John 3:9 has been especially problematic to men and women with sensitive consciences.

In one way or another the teachers in Ephesus believed in what has sometimes been called 'sinning religion'. Their view of human nature apparently made them feel that what John called 'sin' was not sin at all, and that they could have fellowship with God despite the presence in their lives of what John called 'sin'. John does not want to encourage a faith which lightly and easily sins; he writes so that his people will not sin (2:1). Yet he knows that Christians do sin and he also knows that even less-than-perfect Christians may have fellowship with God provided that they 'walk in the light'. An absolute claim to be without sin is to be rejected (1:6-2:2). He expects his people to show love and to walk in the light. He does not expect absolute sinlessness, and he does not want to encourage self-righteousness. They will always need the propitiating blood of Christ.

Now John comes to insist more forcefully that God views sin seriously and that the Christian cannot agree with the gnostics of Ephesus in disregarding the dangers of sin.

---

1. Helen Roseveare, *Give Me This Mountain: An Autobiography* (IVP, 1966), p. 166.

(1) *Sin is living without principle* (3:4). Many trans-lations have 'Everyone who sins breaks the law' and in the next phrase 'Sin is the transgression of the law', or something similar. These references to 'the law' are quite mislead-ing. A more accurate translation is: **Everyone who commits sin also commits lawlessness, and sin is lawlessness**. There is no reference to 'the law' at all! Translations which use the words 'the law' lead the unwary into thinking that there is reference to the Torah here.[2] In fact, John never refers to 'the law' (*ho nomos*). It is also important to note that the Greek has the word for 'also' which many transla-tions omit.

The precise wording ('He who does A, also does B'), leads one to think that there were those who were saying 'what John calls sin is not against any law, is not objec-tionable'. When one recalls the three denials of 1 John 1:6,8,10 it is clear that there were people who were saying 'fellowship is possible without bothering about what John calls sin (*hamartia*)' (cf. 1:6), or 'sin (*hamartia*) does not have any place in our lives' (cf. 1:8), or 'there is nothing we have done that should be called sin (*hamartia*)' (cf. 1:10). They were minimising (cf. 1:6) or denying altogether (1:8,10) the reality of sin in the Christian's life. Their essential statement was: we can commit what John calls 'sin'; there is no law against it.

John's reply is: 'Everyone who practises sin (*hamartia*) also practises lawlessness, and sin (*hamartia*) is lawless-

---

2. See Authorised Version, Good News Bible. New English Bible ('God's law') is ambiguous. Other translations are better (Revised Version, Revised Standard Version, Revised Authorised Version, American Standard Version, Revised Berkeley). The literalism of New American Standard Version is helpful here.

ness'. This is not a reference to the law of Moses, or any
other codified 'law'. It is true that John does say things
about love. He is putting his demands into writing, into
propositional form. But John is not writing a law-code
and does not use the word 'law' at all. His point is that to
sin is to live in an unprincipled way, against the will of
God, against the demand for love. The Christian is free
from the law of Moses, but he is not free from righteousness altogether. He is not free from doing the will of God.
The will of God will outstrip Mosaism. It will go to heights
of love that the Mosaic law never mentioned. Sin is not
transgression of the *Mosaic* law (which encouraged the
slaughter of Canaanites, executed people for walking a
few kilometres on a Saturday, allowed polygamy and relatively easy divorce, demanded Levirate marriage and so
on!). Even the ten commandments are too low a standard
for the Christian.

The force of John's statement is to insist that sin
(*hamartia*) is living in opposition to God's will. *Anomia*
does not have to mean 'transgression of the Torah'; it need
not mean anything more than 'disregard for God's principles of living'. There are plenty of references to 'commands' in 1 John but there never is any citation of the
Torah. The 'commands' are the commands of God mediated through Jesus, focused in the love-command.

(2) *The purpose of Jesus is to remove sin*. John says **⁵And
you know that He was manifested in order to take away sin,
and there is no sin in Him**. Anyone who is careless about
sin is frustrating the very purpose of salvation. God has a
purpose to destroy sin totally. The purpose of salvation
and the fact that God uses a sinless Saviour both show

that God is interested in eventual sinlessness. God is bent upon removing sin now, progressively, day by day. And one day God has plans to remove sin altogether. Both of these facts demonstrate the hostility of God towards sin.

(3) It follows, then, that *the Christian does not have permission to sin*. This seems to be the point of the statement, **'Everyone who remains in Him does not sin**.

This line has been interpreted in many ways. A few say it refers to the removal of sin, to 'perfect love'. Some think it means that the new nature, the regenerate nature of the Christian, is not able to sin. A notable theologian thought it referred to one special kind of sin, the 'sin unto death' (see 5:16). Among evangelicals, however, the dominant interpretation is to emphasize the nature of the present tense of the verbs in this section. Thus Kistemaker translates the verbs in verse 6 as 'keeps on sinning ... continues to sin'[3] and interprets verse 8 in the light of John 8:34, thus implying that 'he who does what is sinful is of the devil' refers to proof of non-salvation as in John 8:44. The possibility of another approach is not considered. An article by V. K. Inman comes to the same conclusion.[4]

This interpretation is so widespread it is worth stating the objections to it. It treats the Greek present tense as though it were a *marked* tense. The difference between marked and unmarked members of a pair[5] is important here. The difference may be illustrated as follows. If I

3. S. J. Kistemaker, *James and I-III John*, (Baker, 1987), p. 297.
4. V. K. Inman, *Distinctive Johannine Vocabulary and the Interpretation of 1 John* 3:9, WTJ, 40, 1977-78, pp. 136-144.
5. See R. A. Close, *English As a Foreign Language* (Allen & Unwin, 1962), pp. 38-43.

say 'My sister lives in India', I am making a present
continuous statement, but the continuity is unmarked,
unemphasized, and I am using a *simple unmarked* tense.
If I say 'My sister is living in India', I am still making a
present continuous statement with an identical meaning,
but now the continuity is marked. The present tense of
Hellenistic Greek may indeed have present continuous
force, but it is not a tense which expresses *marked* continuity. It is a major blemish in the New American Standard
Version that it constantly translates the *unmarked* Greek
continuous tenses as a *marked* continuous tense in English. For example John 7:1 ('And after these things Jesus
was walking in Galilee ...') sounds odd because it translates with a marked tense. The Revised Standard Version,
'Jesus went about in Galilee', is right because the Greek
imperfect is an *unmarked* continuous tense and therefore
requires an *unmarked* English tense such as 'went'. It is a
precisely analogous mistake to translate *hamartanei* as
'keeps on sinning'. The way to *mark* continuity would be
to use an auxiliary verb as Paul does in Romans 6:1. Contrary to many comments on 1 John 3:6 the simple Greek
present does not indicate *marked* continuity.

In any case, this interpretation is difficult to live with
practically. What does it mean to 'keep on sinning'? To sin
once? Twice? Ten times? Some Christians battle with certain sins all of their lives. All Christian have blind spots
and do not recognize aspects of their life as sinful. Or is it a
matter of sinning 'deliberately'? I do not think that any Christian who tries to *live* with this interpretation will find it
very practical. Yet one test of our interpretation of Scripture
is whether it works out practically when we seek to obey
it. God's salvation is meant to be 'worked out' (Phil. 2:12).

The approach that seems to be required by the background to the letter is that the Christian has no permission to sin, may not justify sin, may not be casual about sin. Evidently there were proto-gnostics who disparaged the reality and the significance of sin. The Christian can 'sin', they maintained. 'It is not against any law to sin.' Over and against some such statements John says, 'The Christian does not sin.' This does not seem to mean that he cannot sin, or that he does not sin continuously, or that he does not commit a certain category of sin. In the context of the total letter it must surely mean either *ideally* the Christian does not sin or – as I prefer – the Christian has no *permission* to sin. Christian faith is not 'sinning religion' (as old-time Methodism would put it). If my son wants to do something I do not approve of, I might say, 'No, the Christian does not do that' or 'No, you *cannot* do that.' I do not mean that it is impossible, or that it never happens. I mean that he ought not to do it and I am not giving him permission to do it.

There is a balance between this verse and 1 John 1:8. John is content to leave two contrasting verses in his letter. He cannot bring himself to say, 'The Christian has no sin', but neither can he bring himself to say, 'The Christian life is a sinning life.' He contents himself with making two denials. 1 John 1:8 asks the question: 'Does the Christian sin?' and answers 'Yes!' 1 John 3:4-10 asks the question: 'Does the Christian sin?' and answers 'No!' The balancing statements are not meant to teach perfectionism and introspection. Rather they are meant to give assurance, and to maintain the standard of not-sinning as the Christian goal. 'If any man sin ... we have an Advocate' is counter-balanced by 'I write these things to you so that you do not sin.' It is along such lines that John provides encouragement and incentive at the same time. He sounds like an antinomian but is not; he sounds like a perfectionist but is not. Christian assurance is *vulnerable* to the charge of antinomianism *but is not guilty of it*. Similarly, the call to Christian godliness is *vulnerable* to the charge of perfectionism *but is not guilty of it*.

Questions For Reflection: 1 John 3:4-10

1. Does 1 John 3:4-10 make you feel afraid?
2. What do you think about living practically with the different interpretations of these verses?
3. Is it possible to feel sinful but still have assurance of salvation?

12. Not Sinning (part 2)
1 John 3:4-10

John wishes his friends to set themselves against sin, and reactivate the pursuit of love. Sin is living against God's will (3:4). The purpose of Jesus is to remove sin, and anyone who is careless about sin is frustrating the very purpose of salvation (3:5). Christian faith is not 'sinning religion' (3:6). Now John has further points along the same lines.

(1) *Sin and fellowship with God are incompatible*. John continues: **⁶Everyone who remains in Him does not sin. Everyone who sins has not seen Him and has not known Him**. John is not referring to initial salvation but to current experience of fellowship with God. So if he sees a Christian who is hating his fellow-Christian, by attitude, by lack of compassion, by theft, by immorality, John's analysis is: at the moment you have not seen Him and you have not known Him. He does not say 'has never seen Him, and has never known Him'. 'Seeing God' refers to fellowship. Moses was able to do amazing things for God because he could 'see Him who is invisible' (Heb. 11:27). He was so aware of God, and walked in such fellowship with God, that he was able to live for God despite great   sufferings.

'Seeing God' is physical and this-worldly in 1 John 1:2. It is physical and concerns the final coming of Jesus in 1 John 3:2. But there is also a 'seeing God' which is by faith and takes place in the here and now. Physically 'seeing' Jesus removes sin altogether (3:3), but seeing God with the eye of faith powerfully works against sin even now. Without holiness no-one sees the Lord, even in this

life, and without 'seeing' the Lord there is no holiness.
Fellowship with God works against sin, and sin works
against fellowship with God.

(2) *Character is deducible from behaviour*. John wishes
the idea of 'righteousness' to be firmly placed in the area
of action! So he says **⁷Little children, let no one deceive
you. The one who does righteousness is righteous, just as
He is righteous**. He will not sympathize with the person
who says 'I am righteous in status' without actions corre-
sponding to the claim. He replies: 'The righteousness I
am talking about shows itself in activities of love.' He
expects his people to be like Jesus, not perfectly, not infallibly, but approximately and increasingly. He expects his
people to be like Jesus, in concern, in boldness, in wisdom, in compassion for people, in friendliness, in repudi-
ating revenge, in refusing to discriminate against anyone,
in venturesome actions of love. 'Righteousness' is not a
theological theory. The one who does righteousness is
righteous. What you do is what you are.

(3) *The Christian enterprise involves the destruction of
sin*. John is still speaking to Christians, although he has
the gnostics in mind. **⁸The one who commits sin is of the
devil, for the devil sins from the beginning**. The gnostic teaching is not simply a variant interpretation, a minor 'denomi-
national' difference of opinion among fellow Christians.
Rather, the gnostic teaching is wholly demonic. John is not
actually writing to them. His point is that it is possible for
the devil to find an entrance into the lives of Christians,
and the gnostics are on the side of the devil. The Christian is tempted at times to justify sin, but John says to

him: it is possible for the devil to delude you and trick you into sin. When you sin you are 'of the devil' at that point.

However, John reminds them, **The reason the Son of God appeared was that He might undo the works of the devil** (3:8b). We all tend to think Jesus came simply to *teach* us, to introduce *ideas*. The gnostics especially thought that knowledge was the answer to all problems. But the coming of the Son of God was not simply to introduce academic theories and detached 'ideas'! The coming of the Son of God was with a view to activity. God planned to do something!

Jesus is the eternal Son of God. He was there even before He came, but then He was 'manifested'.

What brought Jesus into the world was the fact of sin. God was determined to take action against all kinds of wrongdoing in His world.

The Christian faith is all about a campaign, a programme of action, in which God plans to destroy sin altogether. It came to a climax on the cross. There the prince of this world was driven out (John 12:31), bound (Luke 11:22), disarmed (Col. 2:15), hurled down (Rev. 12:9). However, the final stages of the victory are still being worked out. Jesus is reigning until all His enemies are defeated. This is the way John's friends must think about the matter. The gnostics want to turn the Christian faith into an academic enterprise. They want to turn the church into a kind of university for the intellectual elites, the people who have their kind of superior 'knowledge'. John says in effect, 'The church is not like a university! It is like a battleground!' We are not taking a theological course! We are in the midst of the greatest battle and conflict that there is. Jesus is not a university lecturer! He is the Captain of the armies of God, the One who has blazed a trail to glory and is summoning us to fight our way through after Him.

So in practical day-by-day life, John's friends must keep in mind what is happening. Jesus is undoing what Satan did. He is undoing the breach of fellowship between mankind and God. He is undoing the kind of hate that came in between Cain and Abel. He is bringing into being a kingdom of light, a realm of holiness, a vast dominion of love, and He is driving back and will one day destroy altogether a kingdom of hate.

(4) *The new birth makes the permission of sin impossible.* John's references to new birth (2:29; 3:9; 4:7; 5:1,4,18; see also John 1:13; 3:6,8) are a piece of picture-language. New birth is what takes place when God puts a 'seed' of life into us. It is a new nature, a new disposition, a new sensitivity to God, a new dynamic which moves in the direction of holiness. It shows itself in a clear understanding that Jesus is the Son of God and the Saviour, and it puts within us affection towards God, a desire for Him. It enables a new willingness to obey him, a willingness which emerges in actual activities of obedience. No-one ever believes, ever repents, ever seeks the life of obedience, ever achieves anything for God, except as the result of this new birth.

The first mark of new birth is heart-gripping faith in Jesus as the Son of God. No-one believes without new birth, and no-one is born again without coming to faith. New birth takes place in connection with God's Word. Generally speaking, God brings people to life and to faith, when His Word is present and is being heard.[1]

---

1. There may be exceptions. 'Infant regeneration' is possible, as Luke 1:15, 41-44 shows.

New birth is entirely an act of God. The teaching concerning predestination is implicit in the teaching concerning new birth. It is 'of His own will' that new life is given
(James 1:18). Yet on the human side it is 'through the word
of truth' (James 1:18). New birth leads away from sinfulness. It is not that it is *impossible* for the Christian to sin,
but it is against his disposition, against the location, the
bearings, the direction, the tendency in which God set his
or her life in new birth. John says, **⁹Every one who is born
of God does not sin, because His seed remains in him, and
he cannot sin, because he is born of God**.

The new birth is permanent. The Christian does not
have easy liberty to sin because 'His seed remains in him,
and he cannot sin, because he is born of God.' There are
some things in the Christian life which can be lost. John
has taught that fellowship can be left behind. Honour at
the second coming of Jesus can be replaced by shame.
The enjoyment of 'remaining' in fellowship with Jesus
can be forgotten. The life of love can be damaged. Compassion towards a brother or sister in Jesus may be
neglected. Even in the judgment day the Christian may
'suffer loss' (1 Cor. 3:15) and the 'prize' may be denied (1
Cor. 9:24-27). Yet there are other things that cannot be
lost and according to John one of them is new birth. It is
this that sets up resistance to sin in the Christian. 'He
cannot sin.' It is not that it is impossible, but it is against
the flow of the way God has made him.

(5) *The new birth is a sign of authentic Christianity*. John
still has his eye on the gnostics. **¹⁰By this the children of
God are manifested and the children of the devil are manifested. Everyone who does not do righteousness is not of**

**God, and nor is the one who does not love his brother or
sister**. Authentic Christianity is a message about new birth
as something that breaks the power of sin. It is 'by this' –
by what he said in 3:4-9 and will say in 3:10b – that
authentic Christianity is recognized. Again (as in 2:5), I
think 'By this' is a vague phrase meaning 'By this matter
that I am talking about now ...'.

The converse truth is that dead, defunct or heretical
Christianity will be marked by disinterest in any message
concerning new birth. It will lack faith in Jesus as the Son
of God come in the flesh. It manifests itself in disregard
of the need of righteousness ('Everyone who does not do
righteousness is not of God'). Supremely it shows itself in
apathy towards the love of the Christian fellowship ('...nor
is the one who does not love his brother or sister').

But where the Christian faith is truly present, it is by
new birth showing itself in deeds of love, that all people
are able to see what is and what is not the gospel of Jesus
Christ. For the gnostics it was knowledge which was the
sign of Christianity. For John it is new birth, faith, and its
end-product, a love within the Christian fellowship which
all people will recognize.

Questions For Reflection: 1 John 3:4-10

1. What is it like to be 'born again'?
2. What are the privileges of being God's sons and daugh-
ters?
3. How can we persuade ourselves and others not to sin?

13. Love (part 1)
1 John 3:11-18

The apostle now develops for the second time (cf. 2:7-11) his teaching concerning Christian love. It will help us if we remember that there are different kinds of 'love', and that John is referring to only one of them.[1] There is sexual attraction, 'the way of a man with a maid' as the Authorised Version puts it (Prov. 30:19). There is affection, the idea that is expressed in the Greek word *storge*, love of family, love of country, love of clan or tribe. There is friendship-love, the kind of love David had for Jonathan, the love that draws people together in companionship, a love that is based on admirable qualities we see in another person, or common interests. None of these is what John has in mind when he speaks of 'love'. He is speaking of *undeserved* love.

Every other kind of 'love' is based on what is seen in the other person. A young person is romantically drawn to another young person because of the kind of sexual chemistry that is between them. *Storge* is rooted in our loyalty to our own kind. Friendship is based on something we have in common with the other person or something that we admire in the other person. Every other kind of love is natural. One does not need to be a Christian to experience sexual attraction or love of friends or love of tribe, but *love* as John uses the word is unmerited love, undeserved love, love that is not caused by anything in the other person. It is the kind of love that was supremely seen in the cross of Christ. God 'so loved' the world in sending Jesus,

---

1. See C. S. Lewis, *The Four Loves* (Fontana, 1963).

but there was nothing in the world to attract God. God was loving the unlovable, the unattractive, the rebellious. This kind of 'love' is unmerited love, love which is not stimulated by the merits of the other person. God's love for the human race is seen in His taking men and women as His children (3:1), and in sending Jesus as the sacrifice for their sins (4:7-8,10,16).

People sometimes call this love *agape*-love because Christians preferred to use the word *agape* ('love') rather than other Greek words that were available. However, we should be careful not to make sweeping claims about the word *agape*. Some might be surprised that it can be used of immoral 'love' (see 2 Samuel 13:15 where *agape* is used in the Greek translation of the Old Testament). However, there is such a thing as unmerited-love, Jesus-love, and it will do no harm if it is specially linked with the word *agape* in the New Testament.

We can look at John's points here under eight headings; the first four of which we shall look at here in chapter 13 and the rest in chapter 14.

(1) *Love is the heart of the Christian message.* Picking up a thought from the end of verse 10, John writes **¹¹For this is the message that you heard from the beginning, that we should love one another**. One could ask, What is the central aspect of the gospel? In one phrase, what is 'the message'? One could say it is the cross of Christ. Paul said: 'God forbid that I should glory in anything except in the cross of our Lord Jesus Christ' (Galatians 6:14; see also 1 Corinthians 2:2). If on God's side the centre of the gospel is the cross of Jesus, on the Christian's side the centre of Christian living is love. 'This is the message ... that we should love ...'.

(2) *God has always been wanting to reverse Genesis 4 as well as Genesis 3. The gospel is the reversal of the Fall.* In Genesis 3:15 the earliest promise of the gospel comes as a promise that God will crush Satan. He will undo everything that Satan had done in engineering an alienation between God and the human race. But Genesis 3 is followed by Genesis 4. The breach between God and man is followed very quickly by a breach between man and woman ('The woman you gave to me...') and then between brother and brother. But Christian love, *agape*-love, **¹²is not like Cain who was of the wicked one and killed his brother**. God is wanting to reverse what Satan did in Genesis 3, and He is wanting to reverse what Satan did in Genesis 4.

(3) *The cause of lack of love is guilt.* John asks, **And why did Cain kill him? Because his works were evil and his brother's were righteous** (3:12b). It was spiritual resentment that led to the murder of Abel. When Cain looked at Abel he felt guilty. Abel was living righteously; Cain was not. Resentment and animosity arose within Cain's heart. Murder was the result. **¹³Do not marvel, my brothers and sisters, if the world hates you**. The same principle that was operating between Cain and Abel will operate between all Christians and the world.

(4) *To lack love is to dwell in a realm of death.* John goes on: **¹⁴We experience that we have passed from death to life, because we love the brothers and sisters. The person who does not love remains in death.**

John has said that sin is lawlessness, refusing to live by good principles of obedience to God's written Word and God's Spirit. The opposite of such 'lawlessness' is not law;

it is love. John is not preoccupied with the Torah or even
with the Decalogue, but is concerned to practise love. John
does not think he is saying anything new (3:11). The
message of Christian love is from 'the beginning', a phrase
which at this point probably refers to the beginning of
human history (John refers to Cain and we know his inclination to use phrases in varied ways). He urges his point
from the Old Testament using the Torah, for Genesis is
part of 'the Torah', but he does not cite the Mosaic institutions (3:12). The hatred he has in mind primarily comes
from 'the world' (3:13), a term which includes the proto-
gnostics; yet his disciples must ensure that they are not so
influenced by the proto-gnostics as to neglect love within
the fellowship and become like Cain who hated his brother.

Verse 14 is one of the major texts used by those who
think that John presents 'tests of life' by which our own
true or false conversion may be assessed. A common line
of approach is that the Christian 'knows (i.e. deduces) that
he has passed from death to life (i.e. that his conversion
has taken place) by self-examination and by seeing (hope-
fully) that he loves the brothers in the Christian community.' If he does not love his brother he 'remains in death'
(i.e. he proves he has not truly become Christian).

But the statement is a positive one: 'we do know that
we have passed from death to life ...'. John is not asking
anyone to question whether they love the brothers; he is
affirming that they do.

Also, in the last phrase he uses the third person: 'anyone who does not love'. He does not say 'Any *of you* who
do not love'. While he evidently does not wish his disciples to be influenced by the false teachers, it is clearly the
opponents he has in mind.

A major question concerns the precise nuance to John's words 'we know'. I have argued that it means 'we experience'. The pathway of love is the key to *experiencing* the fact that the Christian *has* passed from death to life.

Conversely, to fail at the point of love is to 'remain in death' (John 3:14b). Contrary to some exegetical opinion, this need not refer to reversal, to non-salvation. Nor need it refer to proven pseudo-salvation. We notice a change from 'we' to 'he'. It is likely that John has his opponents in mind. Yet that does not mean that this principle is irrelevant to the Christian, for the next verse goes on to speak of 'Everyone'.

What we have here is surely analogous to John's statement already made that the Christian *may* 'walk in darkness' (1:6). The Christian who fails to love is at that point experiencing what he has in principle been delivered from. In the Johannine writings there is always a sharp antithesis between light/darkness and life/death. It would not be possible to take 'death' as *purely and simply* a statement of a lower position of a weak Christian. A realm of lesser salvation is not envisaged for the unloving Christian. It is rather that in one respect the Christian's experience has gone back to that from which he has in principle been delivered. His position as one delivered from the *realm* of the evil one must not delude him into thinking that his manner of life may be taken for granted as all that it should be. He may be 'carnal' in behaviour when he is not 'carnal' in position (see 1 Corinthians 3 and Romans 8 respectively).

John knows about the strange fact that someone who is forgiven and has been delivered from the evil one (2:12-14) may nevertheless be so overtaken in a trespass (to use

Paul's language in Galatians 6:1) that he may for the
moment be experiencing 'darkness' (1:6). He may temporarily be out of fellowship with God and so be experiencing 'death' at this time. This does not have to mean
that his whole position is one of reversal to the realm of
darkness. Nevertheless, until such time as he recovers he
is remaining in an experience that ought not to be his, he
is sharing in something that is characteristic of John's
opponents. He is not being his true self.

John is implicitly rebuking the Christian who says 'But
I have been delivered from darkness.' In a sense John would
agree with this (as 1 John 2:12-14 makes clear), but he
will not allow the Christian to deceive himself. The fact
that one has been removed from darkness to a totally new
realm of light does not mean that it is impossible for darkness to have any influence at all over the Christian. The
unloving Christian may be 'delivered from darkness' in
one sense, but at any given point may be still 'in the darkness' in terms of his current experience.

Questions For Reflection: 1 John 3:11-18

1. Is it helpful to keep in mind different kinds of love?
2. If love is the heart of the Christian message, is it the
same as other faiths?
3. Do we take love for granted? How important is it really?

14. Love (part 2)
1 John 3:11-18

(5) *Lack of love deprives the Christian of the experience of eternal life.* **¹⁵Every person who hates his brother or sister is a murderer and you know that no murderer has eternal life remaining in him**.

1 John 3:15 could be taken as querying retrospectively the genuineness of the Christian's conversion, but two considerations suggest that this would not be the right approach. First, it would make 1 John 2:12-14 meaningless. What is the point of John's striking assertion in 1 John 2:12-14 if some of his readers are simply not Christians at all. Second, one must remember the tension found elsewhere in the New Testament in which a Christian's position as a whole is radically changed, yet he may – as a grotesque anomaly – exhibit characteristics of his old life. The Christian is not 'carnal' but 'in the Spirit' (Rom. 8:5-11). Yet at certain points of his behaviour he may still be 'carnal' (1 Cor. 3:3). Is the Christian carnal? No! May the Christian be carnal at some points of his life? Yes! Is the Christian in darkness? No! May the Christian be in darkness because of his lack of love? Yes! 1 John 3:15b refers neither to loss of salvation nor to proof that claims to salvation have not been valid. Instead, it must be interpreted in terms of the tension between one's having died to sin, and yet needing to die to sin.

In 1 John 3:15 we see an implicit reference to the sixth command of the Decalogue. Yet the Torah is not directly mentioned; the command is put in spiritualised form; it is the reverse of the love-command. By walking in the Spirit the Christian is expected to live out the Decalogue in a

heightened manner, without being under the Mosaic covenant.

Can a Christian hate his brother? John says 'Yes'. When
we allow resentment to rise in our hearts, when we with-
hold forgiveness, when we disregard feelings of compassion, when we resist the promptings of the Spirit to give
help, John calls it 'hate'.

The result in the life of a Christian who tolerates hate
is that his experience of eternal life ceases to operate at
that point. 'Eternal life' is not justification by faith or one's
position as God's elect. Here it surely means the flowing
liveliness that comes from fellowship with God. The Christian who hates will find himself to be powerless, joyless,
feeble in resisting temptation and ineffective in his testimony. The eternal liveliness of the presence of God has
withdrawn because at the moment the Christian is frustrating the purpose of salvation and is living a life of hate.

(6) *Love is defined as sacrifice*. John continues: **¹⁶In this
we know love because he laid down his life for us**.

John invites us to consider Jesus as the model of what
love is. Think of the compassion shown in the cross. There
was nothing attractive in sinners. They were rebellious and
defiant, impure and polluted with self-centredness. Why
should Jesus show such love? But He did.

Think of the sheer sacrifice of the cross. Jesus laid down
His life, quite literally, foregoing the privilege of further
time in this world, handing His life over when He was still
in His thirties.

Think how He sacrificed comfort, how He left aside
opportunities for self-advancement and self-advantage.
Consider how He humbled Himself. It was not simply that

He was *forced* to be humiliated. It was more than that. He humbled Himself! He laid aside the visible glory which He had in heaven. Think how we men and women love to appear glorious in the eyes of others. Who was more glorious than the Son of God? Yet His glory was all laid aside. No-one could tell just by looking at Him who He was. The reason why Judas had to kiss Him to betray Him is that if he had not done so the soldiers would not have known which man was Jesus! His glory was laid aside.

Think of the shame, the insult of the cross. Think of the physical side of it. Think of the spiritual side of what happened. Jesus was in some way abandoned and temporarily lost His life-long fellowship with the Father.

What was it that led Jesus to be willing to do all of this? It was love, sheer love. Love is sacrifice. It is sheer willingness to pour oneself out for the sake of the other person.

John calls us to be like Jesus! The cross is a pattern for us. He says, **And we also ought to lay down our lives for the brothers and sisters** (3:16b). This is one of the most searching and embarrassing texts in the whole Bible. No wonder John has to encourage us in case our hearts condemn us (1 John 3:19-24)! Yet it is a great compliment. To think that God expects me to be like Jesus! I might think this kind of love is simply impossible for me, but God says, 'You can show love like this. You ought to lay down your life for your brothers and sisters.' It means that we leave aside desire for admiration. We leave aside praise and acclamation. We become servants. We accept lack of honour, lack of recognition. We control our tongues, as Jesus, when He was reviled, refused to reply with hate.

(7) *Love is practical compassion.* John says: **¹⁷But whoever has this world's goods and sees his brother or sister in need, and closes his heart from him, how does the love of God remain in that person?** It is noteworthy that John uses the word 'see'. 'If anyone sees his brother ... in need ...' It can be extraordinarily difficult to help needy people. The donor is generally patronizing, easily tricked out of money by people who are surviving quite well, while the genuinely needy say nothing and are neglected. Often an artificial relationship comes into being in which the donor is Mr Bountiful, distributing his largesse, and finding it difficult not to be expressing a spirit of superiority. On the other hand 'the poor' include some very capable people, who are quite skilful at tapping the resources of donors, and the donors do not always possess sufficient discernment as to check where their money is going.

John has at least part of an answer in two of his words: if anyone ... *sees* his *brother* ... The word 'see' and the word 'brother' imply firstly that there is a relationship between the helper and the helped. Secondly, the phrase implies that one person is in close contact with the other. In most 'aid' organisations (and unfortunately in many missionary organisations) there are few close relationships. As John sees the matter, there is already a relationship between brother and brother. When one person is close to the other, he *sees* the need himself. The remedy to the mutual confidence trick that often takes place in 'aid' organisations and missionary organisations is closeness of relationship. Where there is close friendship, where one person is in and out of another person's home, knows his family, has visited his friends and relatives, sooner or later, 'he sees ...'. Personal observation and closeness of fellow-

ship between brothers is the background to the help that
John wants one Christian to give to another Christian. A
man or woman who has close friends among needy Christians, *without* at first giving anything, will eventually 'see'
certain things that will move his heart. His first-hand
knowledge will be the basis of his generosity.

John urges us not to 'shut up the heart'. When we see a
brother or sister in need it is possible to harden ourselves,
to cross the road like the priest and Levite of Luke 10:25-
37. They saw the wounded man but kept away. How often
helping a brother or sister is troublesome, risky, likely to
be misunderstood. And in any case, is the needy person
really a worthy cause? We should ask ourselves were we a
worthy cause when Jesus poured out his soul unto death?

(8) *The call to love has to be faced practically and seriously.* Everything John has said in the paragraph (from
3:11) becomes an exhortation in verse 18: **Little children,
let us not love in word or in talk, but in action and in truth**.
Love has a good reputation. Almost everyone reckons that
love is a good idea. Every religion, every ideology, every
political party, almost every creed of every kind approves
of love. This means that it is very easy to be in love with
the idea of love. Lloyd-Jones actually says 'people who
emphasize love for others in their teaching are those who
of all others must watch that they are not bitter in their
spirit'.[1] It is possible to be quite bitter in denouncing
others for not showing love! A peculiar form of hypocrisy!

John is not interested in talk about love. He is only

1. D. M. Lloyd-Jones, *Children of God* (Crossway, 1993), p. 112.

interested in seeing it in action. It requires thought. 'Love is always highly intelligent'![2] Liking someone is instinctive, almost purely physical. But love thinks. It puts itself into the position of the other person. Love is imaginative, ingenious, inventive. It finds ways of overcoming evil with good. True love is love without play-acting, without wanting to gather a good reputation for being loving. We are to love impartially. We are to love with sensitivity. True love is not talk, not parading benevolence. It is genuine, it is heartfelt without being flashy.

For some of us, it takes a long time before we take love seriously. We say 'Of course, we must show love' and pass on to something more weighty! Sometimes something has to happen to make us face ourselves. Maybe like the twister Jacob we meet a worse twister than ourselves, as happened to Jacob when he met Laban! Maybe someone says some blunt words that, whether he is an enemy or not, we know are true. Maybe suffering has to soften our harsh ways. But one way or another the day has to come when we start taking seriously the need to be a people of love, not talk or subtle pretentiousness, but genuine, Jesus-love.

Questions For Reflection: 1 John 3:11-18

1. Can a Christian hate?
2. Can hate be respectable?
3. Would John agree with Psalm 139:22?

---

2. Lloyd-Jones, *Children*, p. 109.

15. Reassurance (part 1)
1 John 3:19-24

Anyone who seriously sets himself to obey John's call to love is likely to find that his conscience often rebukes him for his failures in love. It is not surprising that 1 John 3:19-24 should follow 1 John 3:11-18.

The unit begins with a call to experience the truth of God by means of love (3:19a) and to overcome the feelings of guilt that arise because of our weaknesses (3:19b-20). It then puts to us the advantages of an uncondemned heart (3:21-22). Verses 23-24a summarise the two commands that are needed: faith and love. Finally verse 24b recalls verse 19a by urging that it is the work of the Spirit to give the experience of being in God.

[19]By this we shall know we are of the truth, and in the presence of God we shall reassure our hearts, [20]in anything in which our hearts condemn us. For God is greater than our hearts and knows everything. [21]Beloved, if our hearts do not condemn us we have boldness before God. [22]And the thing which we ask, we have from Him, because we keep His commandments, and we do the things that are pleasing to Him.

(1) The practice of Christian love leads to the conscious enjoyment of the blessing of God.

When John says 'By this' we find it difficult to discern whether the words look backwards or forwards or whether they are deliberately more general, meaning something like 'By this matter that I am talking about now...'. Sometimes they clearly look forwards (as in 2:3; 3:16), but elsewhere there is a good case for understanding the phrase more generally. This is the case in 3:19. Though love is a way of experiencing the truth of God (a thought which

117

looks back to 3:11-18), it is also true that being able to
rest assured when our hearts condemn us is *also* a way of
experiencing the truth of God (a thought which looks forward to 3:19-24). If 'know' means 'deduce', then the
reader is invited to look to the quality of his love to deter-
mine whether at the present moment he is in fellowship
with God. But as always John's words are deceptively simple. Does verse 19a really mean 'By the quality of our
love we know that we are in a state of salvation'? I have
reservations about people who are so sure that they are
loving that on *that* basis they feel sure they are in a state of
salvation. Or does the phrase mean 'By the quality of our
love we know that the truth is operating in our lives at the
present moment'? That still suggests self-righteousness.

I have suggested before that 'know' often has the sense
of 'experience'. It is by means of love that we experience
the truth of God. Karl Rahner said 'Love is the lamp of
knowledge'. We do not really know the truth of God except in so far as we are showing love. Love has a remark-
able capacity to illuminate. We understand people when
we love them. We get insight into situations when we are
showing love. Conversely, hatred obscures. It prejudices
and blinds and confuses. It is when we are 'rooted and
grounded in love' that we are 'able to comprehend ...' (Eph.
3:17-18). We may paraphrase 1 John 3:19a: 'By this gospel of love and reassurance we come into a rich experience of God's truth.'

(2) The Christian is likely to be attacked by guilt-feel-
ings. John says: **¹⁹By this we shall know we are of the truth,
and in the presence of God we shall reassure our hearts,
²⁰in anything in which our hearts condemn us**. Love brings

us into the experience of God's truth. But it is also true
that when we reflect on the quality of our love we feel
ashamed. How often we have failed! How frail our love
is! What self-centredness there is in each of us! John demonstrates great sensitivity as he continues: '... and in the
presence of God we shall reassure our hearts, in anything
in which our hearts condemn us'. R T Kendall writes that
this 'comes like a breath of fresh air at a time when John
has been so intense'.[1] Even at our best we have matters for
shame when we reflect upon our love of others. This matter of being overcome by guilt feelings is intensified a
thousand times whenever one really seeks to pursue the
pathway of love. Anyone who sets himself to love as Jesus
loved will know what I mean. Lloyd-Jones said that 'if we
set ourselves up, especially as exemplars of this question
of loving the brethren, then we can be sure that the devil
will make a special target of us'.[2] Never is our need of the
mercy of God greater than when we start taking seriously
the need to love our brothers and sisters in Jesus.

(3) Assurance comes by faith in the greatness of God's
mercy. **God is greater than our hearts and knows everything**
(verse 20). The key question is: what is the meaning of the
assertion that 'God is greater than our hearts'? It has been
taken threateningly but it is more likely that it is intended
as encouragement. 'Greatness' in the Old Testament (*godel;
gedolah*) is associated with pride when used of man (Isa.
9:8; 10:12; Ezek. 31:2), but when used of God is related
to God's mercy (Num. 14:19) or great acts of salvation

1. R. T. Kendall, *The Uneasy Conscience*, WR, Winter 1987, p. 3.
2. Lloyd-Jones, *Children of God*, p. 112.

(Deut. 3:24; 5:24; 9:26). When the Psalmist says God's 'greatness' (*gedolah*) is unsearchable, he immediately goes on to speak of God's graciousness, compassion, slowness to anger, greatness in mercy. This is likely to be the background to John's thought here. Sometimes when we seek to live for God and to show love to everyone everywhere we are almost overwhelmed. John is not – as some think – seeking to terrify us into love. That would be a contradiction in terms. How could he talk about reassuring our hearts, in anything in which our hearts condemn us, and then go on to talk about the greatness of God's severity! What would be reassuring about that?

God is greater than our hearts, in mercy, in tenderness, in compassion! Though we may fail in our love, He will not fail in His love. Praise His name! He has more mercy than we realised.

John finds comfort also in the knowledge of God. God has perfect knowledge of humankind. He knows our enemies. He knows the things that bring barriers to love. He knows the way of men and women (Psalms 119:168; 139:3; Job 24:23; Prov. 5:21; Heb. 4:13). He knows our words (Psalms 19:14; 139:4), our thoughts (Psalm 139:2; Luke 11:17; 1 Cor. 3:20), our desires (Acts 1:24; Rom. 8:27).

When we are troubled about situations where we have not shown love, or where we are wrestling day by day with someone who is quarrelsome or who makes arduous demands, we can turn to God and say, 'Lord, I feel so bad, but You know everything!' The knowledge of God is so strengthening. God knows the future (Isa. 41:21-23; 42:9; 46:10; 49:5-7). We can trust Him utterly. We do not trust our own knowledge. We cannot look to our own understanding

(Prov. 3:5, 6). We trust that God knows what He is doing in the world. He sets up times and seasons. He raises one person and puts down another (Dan. 2:21a). We know too that God is able to reveal to us what we need to know. He is worthy of our submission. Often we are fearful of submitting to God. We take the pathway of hostility and quarrelsomeness because we are fearful of the pathway of love. But God knows everything. He can be depended on. God's knowledge is able to comfort us when controversies and disputes and sufferings overtake us. Our hearts may condemn us but we can say 'He *knows* the way I take ...' (Job 23:10); 'the LORD *knows* our frame' (Psalm 103:14).

(4) It is *possible* to be able to handle the matter of doubts and fears, and it is good to do so. It leads to the blessing of boldness in prayer. **²¹Beloved, if our hearts do not condemn us we have boldness before God.** There is nothing more wonderful than to be able to stand before God with boldness. If we go to God but have a feeling that God is unhappy with us, it is terrible. We cannot pray. Within a few minutes we either have to deal with what is making us feel so bad or we have to give up.

How do we overcome the condemning heart? By opening up to Him, trusting His great mercy and realising that He knows everything. We say to Him, 'Lord, You know everything. You know what I said. You know how I got angry. You know how I failed in love towards that person.' How do we overcome the condemning heart? By walking in the light. By total honesty before God. By knowing that we have an Advocate with the Father and that He is the propitiation for our sins. God wants us to have a simple relationship with Him. We are to be confident, child-like in simplicity. God is approachable. Even if we have failed in love – and no-one is likely to be a 100% success – we have a God who is greater than we are. His love will not waver, though our love has failures and gaps.

The result of such love, such confidence in God's great mercy, such dependence on His knowledge, is that we gain power in prayer. Power in prayer does not depend upon the tone of our voice, whether we grovel or whether we are chatty. Power in prayer does not depend upon volume, whether we whisper or whether we shout. Power in prayer depends on whether we are able to come with boldness, and whether God is pleased with us. God is pleased when we are people of love. If your heart condemns you, you need to get back to God speedily, sort out what is making you feel so bad, and get back to being a man or woman of love once again.

Questions For Reflection: 1 John 3:19-24

1. What does the Christian lose by feeling condemned?
2. Is prayer affected by obedience? How obedient do we have to be to get prayers answered?
3. What do you think of Lloyd-Jones' statement on page 119?

16. Reassurance (part 2)
1 John 3:19-24

It is possible for a person to be a true Christian and yet
have a heart which condemns him. Yet this is not totally
disastrous. God is greater than our heart, and our heart
may be more distressed than it need be. When there are
conflicts and quarrels, the Christian invariably feels bad.
The conflict with the gnostics of Ephesus may not have
seemed very 'loving' and John himself has been accused
of being ungracious, even in this letter. Sometimes our
hearts condemn us quite unnecessarily. But even if we are
truly and rightly condemned by our own hearts, there is a
way back. To confess our sins will bring forgiveness and
cleansing, as John has said before (1:7).

But there is something even better. The alternative to
self-condemnation is confidence, and that too is a possibility. John can say, **21Beloved, if our hearts do not condemn us we have boldness before God**. It is not necessary
to have a condemned heart. It is possible to be boldly practising Christian love, boldly trusting in the power of the
blood of Jesus. A combination of bold faith and bold love
will result in a heart that is free from condemnation.

(1) A clear conscience leads to power in prayer. We have
boldness: **22And the thing which we ask, we have from Him,
because we keep His commandments, and we do the things
that are pleasing to Him**. There is such a thing as being so
consciously in the will of God that we are able to pray and
know that God has heard us. In such a spiritual condition
'we have' the things we ask. We have them! There is an
absolute certainty that prayer is answered. One thinks of
Peter at 'the gate called Beautiful' near the temple in

Jerusalem. He passed a crippled man. He has passed him before because every day the Christians were going to the temple (Acts 2:46), and every day the cripple was put there to beg (Acts 3:2). But on this day Peter knew he was being called to do something unusual. He turned to the man, while the man was begging, and said 'In the name of Jesus Christ of Nazareth, walk!' And the man jumped to his feet and began to walk!

Consider Peter's command: 'In the name of Jesus Christ of Nazareth, walk!' It was what James calls 'the prayer of faith' (James 5:15). Peter was not experimenting or hoping that God would hear him. He knew he was in God's will. He knew what would happen. He had a commissioning from God, and with a 100% certainty commanded the man to walk. It was not the kind of thing you do every day, but it illustrates the certainty that comes upon us when we have a totally uncondemned heart.

(2) This kind of life requires the continual practice of faith, love and a clear conscience. We pray with boldness 'because we keep His commandments, and we do the things that are pleasing to Him'. **²³And this is His command, that we believe in the name of His Son, Jesus Christ, and we love one another, as He gave commandment to us**.

Two commands are pressed upon the Christian: the exhortations to faith and love. We might ask: are the two commands of 1 John 3:23 ('that we should believe ... and love') inseparably tied together so that it is not possible to obey (or disobey) the one without the other? There are reasons for thinking that the two commands are in series, with one coming before the other rather than being inseparable and in parallel.

Firstly, John can envisage inconsistent Christians. John affirms that his readers are forgiven and delivered from the realm of the evil one (1 John 2:12-14). The fact that such a statement comes immediately after he raises the possibility of their being in darkness (because of lack of love, 2:11) suggests that his disciples are believers being confused by a new message, but no more than that. They *do* know the truth (2:21), but they are in danger of deception (2:26). John insists that they *are* God's children (3:2). The command to 'believe' (2:23) is one that they have fulfilled; John only wishes to prevent them from drifting into the 'idolatry' (5:20) of a false view of Jesus. Yet the earnestness with which John urges love suggests that their listening to the gnostics has led them to put emphasis on a *gnosis*, an elitist 'anointing' which (so they said) gave a super-spiritual upper-class 'knowledge'. Their being influenced by the 'super-saints' had led to a failure in the realm of love. Admittedly, faith and love are tied together in such a way that if faith is wavering love is affected. But I am suggesting that the two are not so inexorably tied together that it is *impossible* for a believer to lack love. If this were so, John would not need to urge love at all; he would simply urge faith, and love would take care of itself. The fact that his exhortations have two prongs to them suggests that love does not take care of itself and needs *distinct* attention.

Secondly, if this is a correct reading of the matter it means that the order in which John puts the two commands is the logical order. It is faith that prepares the way for love. John's order is 'believe ... love' not 'love ... believe'. It would be hard to imagine that John would have written them the other way round.

A further and related question must be considered: is it right to draw the distinction between an inconsistent Christian and John's opponents, and therefore between inconsistency and (in John's mind) non-salvation? The answer is: John *does* draw the distinction between his opponents and his wayward friends. His opponents are idolaters; his disciples are his 'little children' who must keep away from such idolatry. 1 John 2:19 draws the distinction very starkly. John's opponents have *already* left the Johannine churches ('They went out from us'). They never were believers in the Johannine message. John's 'little children' are in an altogether different category. They are forgiven people who have been rescued from the realm of the evil one (2:12-14). John is not writing to his opponents. He is writing to his friends about his opponents. Yet John does not take it for granted that his opponents have done no damage among his disciples. There may be damaged disciples whose faith is wavering and whose love has been badly affected. John writes to reassure his 'little children' that what they have believed all along is right. They have but to 'abide' in what they first believed. Then they must make sure to walk in the light, and practise love in a practical manner. In so doing they will recover fellowship with the Father and the Son and bring back love into the church.

Christian *self-definition* focuses on Jesus as the Son of God come in the flesh; Christian *progress* focuses upon a second matter: the pursuit of love. Believers in Jesus are required to give themselves to the quest for love, for it is not experienced automatically. The result of such love is, says John, fellowship (3:24a) and the experience of the indwelling Spirit (3:24b).

(3) To live in this way results in mutual indwelling of the Christian and God. **²⁴And the person who keeps His commands remains in God as God remains in him**. 'Abiding' in God is a matter of staying where you are and practising simple obedience. The Greek word for 'abide', as we have seen, means to remain, to stand still, to continue as you are. It is refusing to go beyond Jesus! It is letting Jesus be enough for you. It is saying again and again 'I need nothing except Jesus.' To 'dwell' in God is to stay where He has put you, joined on to the fountain-head of all spiritual blessing and power, Jesus Himself. From that vantage point you simply do everything God tells you. This life of believingly and uncomplicatedly obeying God is what it means to abide in God. The result is God abides in you! You are conscious of His presence. You know He hears your prayers. He provides for you, guides you, stays with you. It all begins with love! All of His commands will be love-commands in one way or another.

(4) The conscious enjoyment of such a relationship leads to an intensified working of the Holy Spirit. **And by this we know that God remains in us, by His Spirit whom He gave to us** (3:24b). I have suggested before that in John the word 'know' tends to approximate to the word 'experience'. John says that by dwelling in God, by keeping all of His love-commands, we *experience* the indwelling of God. This conscious enjoyment of God comes by the working of the Holy Spirit. We *know*, we *experience*, that God dwells in us by the Holy Spirit whom He gave to us. The Holy Spirit is *already* given to us, but there comes what some have called a 'release' of the Holy Spirit.

When the Christian takes love seriously, it is not so

much that the Spirit is 'poured out' on him (Acts 2:17); it is more the Spirit's 'leaping up' in him (John 4:14, New American Bible). Love releases the Spirit. All of the promises about the Spirit are activated. There comes boldness to witness. You are afraid of no-one when you love them. There comes joy unspeakable and full of glory. The first part of the fruit of the Spirit (love) is followed by the second part of the fruit of the Spirit (joy).

You see it in the life of Jesus. He would call God 'Abba' in prayer because welling up within Him was the consciousness that God was His Father. He was very conscious of the anointing of the Spirit and knew it was His enabling to do the work of the Father. 'The Spirit of the Lord is upon me,' he said. It was conscious and experiential. He knew!

This is one of the greatest discoveries of the Christian life. Love releases the flow of the Holy Spirit.

Questions For Reflection: 1 John 3:19-24

1. If our hearts condemn us what can we do about it?
2. How is praying affected by the feeling of our hearts?
3. Is it possible to have faith without love? Is it possible to have love without faith?

17. Testing the Spirits (part 1)
1 John 4:1-6

In every age of the Christian church there have been those who claim direct revelations from God. There is nothing wrong with that, in itself. Paul says Christians may come to the Christian meeting bringing 'a revelation' (1 Cor. 14:26). But claims to revelation are numerous and often contradictory. Clearly the gnostic heretics in Ephesus were claiming 'revelations' in support of their false teaching. Today also, many will step forward making claims that they are the mouthpiece of God. This is not completely wrong; many preachers (including myself) often feel that God is giving them what to say. Yet heavy claims to messages from God give the church of Jesus a major responsibility, that of discerning true claims amidst false.

It is not a new problem today and it was not a new problem in the days of the New Testament. Hundreds of years before John's time, in the days of Ahab, four hundred prophets predicted success for Ahab and one prophet predicted failure (1 Kings 22:1-28). How was it possible to know which was true? Jeremiah's prophecies were constantly opposed by those who brought contrary messages.

It is worth noting what John does *not* do to handle this problem. First, he does not seek to kill the entire issue of prophetic disclosures by squashing all revelations. He did not say, 'There is no such thing as direct revelation from God.' John never questioned the reality of revelations from God. There would be little point in his saying 'Test the spirits' if all claims to revelation were false. One only needs to test revelations if some of them are true. John's difficulty was not that prophetic claims were being made, but

rather how to help Christians to find their way between
the true and the false. He does not say 'Believe not *any*
spirit ...', but 'Believe not *every* spirit ...'.

Secondly, John did *not* handle the problem by restricting revelation to the leadership or an apostolic elite. It is
true that in John's thinking apostolic eyewitness testimony
concerning the reality of Jesus' humanity is a vital basis
to the gospel (see 1:1-4), but he did not urge that *only*
apostles have revelations. John is rather different in his
handling of the matter from Ignatius who had to face the
problem a few years after John (maybe about 20 years
later). Ignatius' way was to emphasize the official minis-
tries of the churches.

Thirdly, John's appeal to them to test revelations is similarly not addressed to church leaders only. He is addressing his letter to all the Christians. He expects the believers, in fellowship together, to be discerning. No doubt there
is leadership within the total community, and there is obviously the leadership of John himself, but the ordinary
believer is not excluded.

John asks his readers to test revelations that claims to
be from God. First he makes a general appeal: the spirits
must be tested. It is not examination of one's status before
God that is envisaged but examination of what claims to
be prophetic word (4:1).

Then he mentions one test that was crucial in the situation in which John found himself: orthodoxy concerning
the Son of God who has come to this world in genuine
human flesh. They must test all prophecies with the test
concerning the person of Jesus Christ (4:2-3).

Then he expresses his confidence in them. He has
something to say about the Christians at Ephesus (4:4),

something to say about the gnostics (4:5), and something to say about himself and his fellow apostles (4:6).

First, *we consider his general appeal*. **¹Beloved, do not believe every spirit, but test the spirits to see whether they are of God, because many false prophets have gone out into the world**. Behind every prophecy is a spirit. There are prophecies that come from the Holy Spirit of God. There are prophecies that come from the person's own mind, a 'deceit of the heart' (Jer. 14:14). Worse still there are 'deceiving spirits and doctrines of demons' (1 Tim. 4:1).

What kind of tests did John have in mind? The next verse goes on to specify one, but he may have had others. There are a further five I want to suggest.

(1) *Non-fulfilment*. Often prophecies have a predictive element. If the prediction does not come true, it was a false revelation. Micaiah said: 'If you ever return in peace, the LORD has not spoken by me' (1 Kings 22:28). Four hundred prophets were proved false. 'If the thing does not happen ... the prophet has spoken it presumptuously' (Deut. 18:22).

(2) *Influence for good or evil*. True revelation leads to righteousness, a point John is often making. It is after a call to godliness (Matt. 7:13-14) that Jesus warns of false revelation (Matt. 7:15) and says 'You will know *them*' – the false prophets – by their fruits' (Matt. 7:16-20). Jeremiah complained that false prophets always said 'Peace, peace ...' and sought to nullify Jeremiah's message about the chastening coming upon Israel because of the nation's sin.

(3) *Orthodoxy*. Deuteronomy 13 warned that if a prophet encouraged the people to go after a god other than the LORD, the God of Israel, he should be executed. This is the

point that John will come to shortly. After his general
appeal ('Test the spirits') he will come to one specific test
for the particular crisis facing the churches, that of orthodoxy concerning the person of Jesus Christ (4:2-3).

(4) *The prophet's motivation.* Prophesying can be a
financially rewarding business. Paul warned against 'ped-
dling' the Word of God (2 Cor. 2:17) and handling the
Word of God deceitfully (2 Cor. 4:2). One must be careful
of the kind of preacher who is exceedingly concerned that
'the offering' should come in his direction!

(5) *Eccentricity.* Bizarre and eccentric claims to revelation are to be viewed with caution. Satan urged Jesus
to turn stones into bread and suggested a suicide-leap from
the pinnacle of the temple. The very eccentricity of the
advice was a hint that it was phoney. Admittedly, it must
be recognized that God can use very odd characters. God's
leaders in Scripture sometimes have unusual callings.
Think of Hosea being called to marry a 'wife of harlotry'
(surely, quite literal!), Isaiah being called to walk naked,
Ezekiel being told to cook with dung, and so on. Unusual
characters are not necessarily false. Yet eccentric advice
ought to flash warning lights in our mind. The more
eccentric the person, the more the impact of the teaching
must be tested. If he passes every other test his eccentricity
may be part of his call. But sometimes eccentricity is the
prelude to something worse. It is not so much the eccentricity of the *person* that matters; it is the oddness of the
counsel that must be treated with care.

It is worth mentioning what is not a test of true prophecy. 'Signs and wonders' are not a test! Deuteronomy
warned about a prophet who would come 'and he gives
you a sign or a wonder' (13:1). Even if the sign or the won-

der does come to pass, if it is against orthodox teaching
and orthodox living the prophecy is not to be received.

Lloyd-Jones' book, *Prove All Things*[1], gives many practical pieces of advice in connection with this subject. He
warns against trusting feelings too much, even feelings of
love for God. He invites us to be willing to think, to be
well-taught by the Scriptures. He warns against prophecies that are predictive. It is not that they are impossible;
but they require special care. What contradicts Scripture
must be rejected. Excessive claims to direct guidance,
anything that makes 'self' predominant, the prominence
of a 'physical' element, all have dangers attached to them.
And Lloyd-Jones warns against the power of suggestion.

However, no-one will be so clever in 'testing the spirits' that he or she makes no mistakes. In the midst of
revival mistakes are often made. He who never made a
mistake never made anything! Sometimes, in the liveliness of revival, eccentricities have to be tolerated. Things
will balance out eventually if the revival is real. John 16:13
says: 'When the Spirit comes He will guide you into all
the truth.' It does *not* say: 'When the truth comes it will
guide you into knowing the Spirit.' One tends to feel that
God honours the truth, and therefore that it is the truth
which leads us into the experience of the Spirit. This is
true, but John 16:13 puts it the other way round. Over the
years one has noticed churches which have majored on
the truth but the truth does not seem to have led them into
the Spirit.

On the other hand, one notices churches that seem genu-

---

1. D. Martyn Lloyd-Jones, *Prove All Things,* Kingsway, 1985. I give
an outline of Lloyd-Jones' teaching in this respect in my *Baptism with
the Spirit: The Teaching of Martyn Lloyd-Jones* (IVP, 1989), pp. 156-157.

inely to have the Holy Spirit and yet hold teachings that
verge on the cultic. As the years go by, the cultic elements
fall aside and they get a stronger and stronger grasp of the
gospel. The 'sound' churches often do not seem to get the
Spirit, but the 'semi-cultic' Holy Spirit churches, in most
cases, do eventually seem to drop aside their fads and end
up preaching a balanced gospel.

We must 'test the spirits' but not get so uptight that, if
something new happens and the Holy Spirit is at work, we
are so careful that the Holy Spirit fails our tests! We must
test all things, but at the same time let God be God. And
God has a habit of being a God of surprises!

One test, however, is head and shoulders above everything else. **²By this you shall know the Spirit of God. Every
Spirit that confesses Jesus Christ come in the flesh is of
God. ³And every spirit which does not confess Jesus is not
from God. And this is the spirit of Antichrist, concerning
which you heard that it was coming, and now it is already in
the world**. There can never be an authentic gospel without
a true teaching concerning Jesus, the Son of God come in
the flesh. Any true gospel must at the very least boldly
blaze abroad that the man Jesus is 'the Christ', the divine
Saviour. The Son of God has come *in the flesh*. He is as
much God as the Father is God. He is as much human as
we are human, in all things except sin. Only such a One
can be our Saviour.

Questions For Reflection: 1 John 4:1-6

1. Do we need to test the spirits today?
2. List some more ways of testing the spirits.
3. Is it possible to make the tests too easy? Too difficult?

18. Testing the Spirits (part 2)
1 John 4:1-6

As we noted in the previous chapter, John has something to say about three groups of people: the Christians in Ephesus, the gnostics, and lastly himself and his fellow-apostles. Let us look at what he says about each group.

(1) John is quite confident that all will be well with his friends in Ephesus. He encourages them by telling them so. **'You are of God, little children, and you have conquered them, because greater is He who is in you than he who is in the world**.

John tells them that they do have the truth. Christians can be intimidated by the boastful claims of false prophets. 'We have knowledge,' said the ancient gnostic, and many weak Christians were inclined to believe them. 'No intelligent person can really believe...'. Boastful claims to possess knowledge were as common in the ancient world as they are now, but John says, 'Don't let yourself be intimidated by the gnostics. *You* are of God'; the Greek word for 'you' is emphasized. It is not those gnostics who have knowledge of God; it is *you*. Actually John should not have needed to say this. They had the anointing of the Holy Spirit and deep within they *knew* they were right. But 'modern knowledge' can be very intimidating to weak Christians. Sometimes there is a need for someone who will stand up and boldly declare what the gospel is. This is where the apostle John came in. Sometimes a pastor needs to reassure his people: 'You *are* saved. God *is* using you. What you believe is *right*.' And the Christian is strengthened by someone whose judgment he values, affirming him and telling him that he is right to do what he is doing.

They have already won a victory. The gnostics were still around and no doubt they were very vocal, but John is able to say, 'You have overcome them.' They may seem very self-confident, says John, but when you stood firm by what you knew was right and they left your churches (2:19), at that point you were actually overcoming them.

God was in them. The Christians at Ephesus were living in the aftermath of a controversial time when false teachers had been trying to shake them from what they knew to be true. The Christians had got a victory, but it seems that they did not feel very victorious. John says that they did get victory over them. The future of the church had been preserved.

The enemies of God's people act as if they have super-intelligence, but in due time they simply crumble. Think of all the great enemies that the church of Jesus has faced: persecution, the tyranny of antichristian rulers who have opposed Christians, the opposition to the church of Jesus that has arisen in the name of science or tolerance or modern knowledge. It goes on for centuries. One adversary after another is raised up by Satan, the enemy of the church.

But century after century the people of God stand strong and come through. 'Greater is He who is in you than he who is in the world.' Jesus will bring His church through every attack. We do not need to succumb to modern antichristian philosophies, even when they disguise themselves as 'modern' forms of the Christian faith. They will collapse in due course, and the humble Christian who believes the original and only gospel will come through victoriously.

(2) John has something to say about the gnostics. **⁵They are from the world, so they speak from the world and the world hears them**. They claimed their teaching came from superior knowledge and from special revelations that were not available to 'ordinary' people.

Modern 'gnostics' are the same. They make claim to superior knowledge. 'We are "scientific",' they say. 'The church ought to abandon its supernaturalism and get on with helping to improve society!' So they say! 'We have modern knowledge and we know that all this stuff about the Son of God come in the flesh is not really what is needed. Why don't you ...?' And they go on to tell us of their foolish suggestions about how to improve the church!

John has some comments to make about the ancient gnostics and he would say the same things today.

Firstly, the 'revised' gospel they are presenting, he would say, is no gospel at all. The gospel starts with the basic facts about what God has done. Jesus is the Son of God! He has come in the flesh. He died. He rose again. He is alive today. He is coming again. He pours out the Spirit. These are facts. No amount of philosophical or theological theorising will change these basic facts of the gospel. They may want to talk about 'The new theology' (as they did at the beginning of the twentieth century), or 'The myth of God incarnate' (as they did in the 1970s), but unless their gospel starts with some basic facts about what God has done they have no gospel at all.

Secondly, this revised gospel, says John, is worldly. You may have a great brain. You may sit in your study, in some magnificent university, and write books about your ideas concerning religion and theology. The students will flock to you to write their theses while they imbibe your

great ideas. But the whole enterprise is worldly! It is trying to combine human research, human philosophy,
human ideas, with the gospel of God. The result is that the
gospel is covered up and only man-made ideas are left.
The one-and-only gospel is supernatural. It begins with
an incarnation, with God come in the flesh! It is supernatural. It is revealed. It is the power of God for salvation
for everyone who believes it. Take it or leave it. We Christians have taken it and the Son of God has changed our
lives and given us the power of the Holy Spirit. We *do*
know God, and we know that we do.

Thirdly, of course it is revised 'gospels' that will be
popular with the world. The world is quite happy with its
own ideas dressed up in gospel-language. No wonder the
world is quite tolerant of modern substitute gospels. These
are only their pagan philosophies rearranged and presented
to them again as if they were the gospel. The 'gnostics'
were the most 'advanced' thinkers of their day, but the
inspired apostle John, an eyewitness of the resurrection of
Jesus from the dead, says about them: 'They are from the
world ...'.

(3) John has something to say about himself and his fellow apostles: **⁶We are of God. The person who knows God
hears us, and whoever is not from God does not hear us.
From this we know the Spirit of truth and the spirit of error.** By 'we' he seems now to mean 'we apostles', because
he used the word 'you' when talking of the Christians at
Ephesus in verse 4. The false teachers are 'they'. 'We'
means the apostle John and his fellow apostles and col-
leagues, the ones who had proclaimed the gospel message
at the beginning.

The authentic Christian is a person who hears the revelation that comes via Jesus, from the original first-generation apostles. It may seem arrogant to say 'the person who knows God hears us'. Someone might want to say 'But that is what all religions say!' But we must remember that John's message did not *begin* simply with claims to an interior revelation. It began with something outside, something anyone can investigate, 'that which was from the beginning, which we have heard, which we have seen with our eyes, which we have beheld and our hands have handled'. John began with talking about eyewitness testimony to a person who was raised from the dead.

In addition, one must remember that John saw the glory of Jesus on the mount of transfiguration. There is no point in someone who has *seen* the glory of God in Jesus presenting the gospel as though it were just one option among many.

Then one must remember that John was one of those who received the power of the Holy Spirit on the day of Pentecost. You can hardly expect someone who was baptized with the kind of power and illumination that came upon John by the Holy Spirit to be using 'ifs' and 'maybes' and 'perhaps'. John knows!

In the same way the modern Christian can use similar language. The outside world finds it hard to understand, and authentically Christian language must seem a bit arrogant. But there is not much we can do about it! When God speaks He is capable of speaking in such a way that we know we have heard Him! All we can do for friends who think we are arrogant is to remind them that we are pointing to historical facts that can be investigated. The resurrection of Jesus can be investigated. The origin of

the Christian church can be investigated. The power of the
Holy Spirit can be known by coming to Jesus! The historical facts of the gospel are there for anyone to investigate
who wants to, yet there is an even greater way. God is
there. God is close to us. He is the one who sustains life
and arranges our existence. He invites us to 'feel after'
Him or 'grope after' Him (Acts 17:27). God is not very
far away. Even pagan Greeks were expected to feel after
Him. With the much clearer revelation we now have about
Jesus, God is nearer than ever. He is able to be found.
When we find Him, we shall know! Then we shall discover
what John meant. The person who knows God hears us.

The opposite is true. The gnostics were not Christians.
They would not listen to John. Of course not! They did
not have the anointing of the Holy Spirit. Whoever is not
from God – John is thinking of gnostic teachers – does not
submit to the revelation that came through the apostles.

This is the dividing line between a true and a false
gospel. Fake Christianity does not submit to John and his
fellow apostles. It does not submit to the New Testament.
This is the key to the whole matter. From this we know the
Spirit of truth, the Holy Spirit, and the spirit of error,
Antichrist, the enemy of Jesus.

Questions For Reflection: 1 John 4:1-6

1. Should we sometimes rely on the confidence of others?
2. Are there versions of Christian faith which the world
likes?
3. Can the modern Christian speak like John: 'The person
who knows God hears us'?

19. Love (part 1)
1 John 4:7-12

For the third time John focuses on love (after 2:7-11; 3:11-18). Consciously or unconsciously, he starts a third cycle of meditations. Before he said that love was an old commandment (2:7) and a new commandment (2:8a) at the same time. It is seen in Jesus and is characteristic of the Christian because it is an essential ingredient of the new days of God's kingdom (2:8b). It is the central aspect of the light of God, the opposite of hate which is darkness (2:10). Love – said John – illumines, but hate brings confusion (2:11).

Then in 3:11-18 he returned to the theme. The world is a realm of hate, he said. From the beginning there was antagonism between hatred and love. Tension between the world and God's people is only to be expected (3:11-13). The experience of God's life comes through love (3:14-15), the essential characteristics of which are sacrifice (3:16), compassion (3:17) and reality (3:18).

Now again John urges love (4:7-12), building on what he has said.

Firstly, John writes that *the God of the Bible is the only source of love*. There are of course different kinds of love, but with regard to the kind of selfless concern for people that John has in mind, one must say that God, as known in Jesus, is its only source. **⁷Beloved, let us love one another, for love comes from God**.

Secondly, John writes that *love requires new birth*. No-one is able truly to show this kind of love except by being 'born again'. John continues: ... **and everyone who loves is born of God** ....

141

Thirdly, John writes that *love is essential to fellowship with God*. **Everyone who loves is born of God and knows God**. Love not only shows to others that the person is born of God, it also means that the Christian's knowledge of God is currently being enjoyed. John distinguishes the two. His readers are born of God, yet he writes to restore fellowship with the Father and the Son. The two are not inexorably intertwined, otherwise there would be no need for the epistle. Love arises from and demonstrates two things: new birth and its development, fellowship with God.

Verse 8 takes up the last thought of verse 7: **The person who does not love has not known God, because God is love**. 'The person who does not love' may still be a Christian (for every Christian has had times when he has not shown love). John is not denying anyone's Christian conversion. His point is rather that at that point in their life no knowledge of God is operating. John explicitly does not say that lack of love is proof of not having been begotten of God. He cannot say that, for that would imply that it is *impossible* for the Christian not to love. John knows only too well that some of his little children have fallen into lovelessness. Yet he does not deny the reality of their first faith.

There is a tradition in the interpretation of 1 John which seems to want the unloving Christians to deny what has already happened in their lives ('that which you heard from the beginning'). But John does not want them to deny what happened 'in the beginning' of their Christian pilgrimage; he wants them to go back to it and recover it. 'You never had anything', says one kind of exposition. 'Regard your conversion as false and seek true conversion.' John says: 'Your conversion was real enough. But at the mo-

ment you are in darkness. You had your life right when
you first believed. You are making a mistake if you are
thinking the proto-gnostics may be right and if you are
considering moving from Jesus as you knew him. Go back
to what you had from the beginning.' There are similar
appeals in the book of Revelation: 'You abandoned the
love you had ... do the works you did at first.' 'Strengthen
what remains ... Remember what you received and heard.'
'Hold fast what you have' (2:4, 5; 3:2, 3, 11). John says,
in effect, 'Only in such a way will you recover your fellowship with the Father and the Son.' The difference between the two kinds of exposition is that some expositors
want to deny the authenticity of past knowledge of Jesus
in inconsistent Christians. But John does not deny their
past knowledge of Jesus and he wants to call them back to it.

John structures his remarks in verses 7-8 in a way that
explicitly underlines this aspect of the matter. For (as
Brown notes) the chiasmus of verses 7-8 is not perfect. It
might be expected to read:

Everyone who loves	*One who does not love*
has been begotten of God	has known nothing of God
and knows God	and has not been begotten of God.

Instead it reads:

Everyone who loves	*One who does not love*
has been begotten of God	has known nothing of God
and knows God	for God is love.

In the place where one might expect 'and has not been
begotten of God' one finds simply 'God is love'.[1] This is

---

1. Brown, *Epistles*, p. 548.

precisely what one would expect if John did not maintain
that new birth infallibly and inexorably produces love.
Brown comments: 'The God of love cannot beget children
who do not love.'[2] But this ties love and new birth together
too tightly. Is it impossible for a Christian to be unloving?
One has two thousand years of church history to prove
otherwise! Brown's observation is too strong. It should
have read: 'The God of love begets children with the *ability*
to love.' In John's thinking it would not be possible for a
non-Christian to show true love until he has come to new
birth. With the new birth comes, in John's mind, the ability to love. Yet even then love is not an automatic matter. It
has to receive deliberate attention from the Christian. John
is both demanding and gracious at the same time. He lives
with an antinomy: 'I write to you to tell you not to sin'; 'If
anyone sins we have an advocate ... He is a propitiation'.
Anyone who fails to love contradicts his new birth; yet
contradiction of the new birth is a possibility and John
says nothing to imply that it is impossible for a Christian
to lack love. (Is it not self-righteousness to think otherwise? Who, knowing himself, could think differently?)

God is love, says John (4:8). One might ask: is this the
whole truth? Does the Bible not say 'God is light', and
does it not also speak of the wrath of God? However, the
wrath of God and the love of God are not parallel. The
Bible never says 'God is wrath'; it does say 'God is love.'
To put it the other way round: the Bible never says 'God
began to love'; it does say 'God became angry.' The Bible
portrays God as love in and of Himself; but His wrath is
always a *re*-action.

---

2. Brown, *Epistles*, p. 548, n. 12.

The love of God! It is love for which one can give no reason in ourselves, the love that is staggeringly undeserved. It is the love that is a mighty Conqueror. It overcomes the problem of sin, which was so great a matter that it was a problem even to God Himself! It is love, the reasons for which are in God alone. 'The LORD set his love on you ... because the LORD loves you!' (Deut. 7:7-8). It is the love which is inexplicable, causeless, spontaneous, free. It is God's generosity, His willingness to give and give and give, His willingness to pay any price in order to give. It is His identifying with the other person, His taking thought about all their deepest needs. It is His determination to deal kindly with us no matter what we do. It is His determination to take the initiative, His reluctance to stop speaking to us, His purpose to overcome every barrier, His freeing us from our deepest predicaments, His resolve to rescue us from the plights and distresses and the anarchies that flow from our ingrained and inherited sinfulness.

The songwriters put it best. It needs music and poetry to express the feelings and the admiration that rises in our hearts. 'Love found a way', says the songwriter.

> Love found a way to redeem my soul
> Love found a way that could make me whole.
> Love sent my Lord to the cross of shame.
> Love found a way, O praise His holy name.

Seth Sykes and his wife spoke of

> Love, oh, the wonderful love,
> The love of God to even me.
> Love, wonderful love, so great, so rich, so free.

> Wide, as wide as the ocean,
> Deep, as deep as the sea,
> High, as high as the heav'ns above,
> His love to me.

Others write of how they found this love and experienced it in Jesus.

> O Christ, in Thee my soul hath found,
> And found in Thee alone,
> The peace, the joy I sought so long,
> The bliss till now unknown.
>
> I sighed for rest and happiness,
> I yearned for them, not Thee;
> But while I passed my Saviour by,
> His love laid hold of me.
>
> I tried the broken cisterns Lord,
> But, ah! the waters failed!
> E'en as I stooped to drink they fled,
> And mocked me as I wailed.
>
> Now none but Christ can satisfy,
> None other name for me.
> There's love and life and lasting joy,
> Lord Jesus, found in Thee.[3]

But, says John, 'If God loved us in this way, we ought also to love one another' (4:11). Our love must 'find a way' to

---

3. Wonderful love that rescued me..., Love wonderful love..., O Christ in Thee..., *Redemption Hymnal*, 655, 514, 499.

make people whole and free them from shame. Our love
must be wonderful love, so great, so rich, so free, wide, as
wide as the ocean, deep, as deep as the sea, high, as high
as the heavens above. Our love must give peace to others,
joy to others, 'love and life and lasting joy'. God's love to
us is to become – says John – God's love through us.

Questions For Reflection: 1 John 4:7-12

1. 'Love is the lamp of knowledge.' Does this make sense?
2. 'The God of the Bible is the only source of love'? Is this
true?
3. How can the Christian regain love?

20. Love (part 2)
1 John 4:7-12

John is still pursuing his exhortation: 'Beloved, let us love one another, for love comes from God' (verse 7). Now he goes on to point to the demonstration of love in the sacrifice of Jesus (4:9) and in the initiative of God (4:10). This obliges love (4:11). Verse 12 makes the point that the invisible God only becomes manifest in the life of love. The experience of the indwelling of God comes about only in the life of love. Love is thus 'perfected'.

First, he puts to us *the demonstration of love in the sacrifice of Jesus*. He says: **⁹By this the love of God is revealed among us, that God sent His one and only Son into the world in order that we might live through Him**. How do you measure love? One way is to consider whether it shows itself, whether it takes any action. God's love is manifested, revealed. It is not simply a theory or a hidden feeling in God. It has revealed itself in what He has done for us.

How do you measure love? Another way is to consider how much it is willing to do, how much trouble it will take, how great a sacrifice it will make. God's love was manifested in His sending Jesus to this world. Who was Jesus? He was 'the one and only Son'. Jesus was the 'Son of God' in a unique way. He knew it Himself. He loved to call God 'Abba', a very intimate word almost meaning 'Daddy', and spoke of God as 'My Father' and of Himself as 'the Son' (Matt. 11:27; Luke 10:22). He used the expression 'the Son' as a title (Mark 13:32) and regarded 'the Son' as more than any other servant of God (see Mark 12:1-12).

John was more far-seeing than many New Testament
writers in comprehending what it means for Jesus to be
the 'one and only Son'. It implies that in some way Jesus
existed as the 'Son of God' before He was born. God sent
one who was *already* His Son (John 3:16). His Sonship
preceded His being sent. According to John 5:19-27 the
Father and the Son are equally honoured (5:23) and are
equally the object of faith (5:24). Because Jesus used
Father-Son terminology, Jewish people rightly took Him
to be claiming deity (John 5:18). The Son and the Father
are one (John 10:34-36). In 1 John also 'Sonship' precedes Jesus' coming to earth. The Lord Jesus Christ was
eternally God's Son; there came a point where He was
'sent' and became man. If love is measured by the value
of what is given, then how much God loved us in not with-
holding His unique and divine Son.

How do you measure love? In a situation of dispute
and quarrel, love is measured by asking which side takes
the first step to bring about reconciliation and harmony.
In the case of human salvation, the human race took no
initiative at all. **[10]In this is love, not that we loved God but
that He loved us**.... Men and women did not reach out after
God at all in true worship and gratitude. Although they
knew that God was there they did not glorify Him as God
and they were not in any way grateful to Him (see Rom.
1:21). The initiative was entirely on God's side. He took
the steps that were needed to bring us to Himself. The
purpose was 'that we might live through Him'. When we
are cleansed from our sins the result is the spiritual liveliness that comes from God.

How do you measure love? In how much someone is
willing to suffer to bring about a right situation. So how

much was God willing to do, how much trouble was He willing to take, how great a sacrifice would He make John answers ... **He loved us, and sent His Son as the propitiation for our sins**. The human situation was awful. God was righteously angry with the human race. But God sent His Son to be a 'propitiation'. Although the meaning of the word has been much discussed, there can be little doubt that it includes the notion of turning away anger. Propitiation is 'a sacrifice that turns away anger'.

God is love; but there is such a thing as the anger of God. It is not a matter of God losing His temper. There is no loss of control when God is angry (as in human anger, generally). It is never an 'explosion'; it is never unpredictable; it is never without warning. It is one of God's perfections. It can be seen in human government (Rom. 13:4,5), in history (Rom. 1:18; 9:22; 1 Thess. 2:16; Heb. 3:11; 4:3). It will be displayed in the day of wrath (Matt. 3:7; Rom. 2:5-11). It is roused by sin (Eph. 5:3-6; Col. 3:5,6), especially the sin of idolatry (Deut. 6:14ff; Josh. 23:16).

God's anger is His purposeful reaction to sin and evil, by means of which He wishes to express His revulsion and call people to repentance. In Exodus 32:10, God says, 'Let Me alone ... that My wrath may burn hot...'. God's anger is purposeful; it is a decision.

God's anger is a *re-action*. It is not inherent and spontaneous, as is His love. Love in God is eternal. But wrath does not belong to His very being in the way that love does. His wrath is never spontaneous. He *becomes* angry; He is love (see Num. 11:1; Psalm 2:10-11).

God's anger is holy anger. It burns when holiness is scorned (Exod. 32:10ff; Isa. 5:25). God's anger is injured love (Heb. 10:31). It is the result of human unfaithfulness

(Psalm 78:7-60; Judg. 2:10-22). God's anger is open to
being turned aside. It is only when we resist God's love
that God's anger becomes final, and destructive and disastrous for us.

'Propitiation' means that in some mysterious way God's
anger against sin fell upon Jesus instead of on me. Because
God sent His Son to be a 'propitiation', God does not
reject me on account of my sins, for on the cross He
rejected Jesus instead. The Christian is delivered from
God's anger. Although God can show fatherly displeasure
when the Christian sins, yet the Christian is delivered for
all time from the realm of sin and judgment. God's wrath
no longer threatens Him (Rom. 3:25; 5:9; 1 Thess. 1:10;
5:9).

This is God's love. Despite all of His holy revulsion
against sin, despite the fact that His nature rises up in
hatred against all that is contrary to His will, He found a
way for us to be His children. In some mysterious way
God punished our sins in Jesus, so that they might not be
punished in us.

John says all this not simply to give us assurance of
salvation and acceptance, although that is precisely what
his words do, but for a further reason. The treatment God
has shown us John now wants us to show each other. If the
Father has turned aside His own wrath from us, John wants
us to turn aside our wrath from others. **11Beloved, if God
loved us in this way, we ought also to love one another**. God
could have let the weight of His anger fall upon us, but He
found another way. It is as though He stopped Himself
and gave further thought to the matter (if, as the Bible
allows, we may think about it in a very human way). Instead of consuming the human race in His displeasure He

showed love to the entire human race and sent His Son.

Now, says John, you do the same thing! Instead of reacting in wrath towards people, hold back. Find a way to break through in love. Find a way in love of overcoming the sin of the other person. Conquer the sinful resentments and animosities in yourself. Overcome the envy, the vindictiveness, the irritability, the impatience, that you feel towards the other person. And remember who you are! Think of what A. W. Tozer called your 'hyphenated sins': self-centredness, self-consciousness, self-defensiveness, self-exaltation, self-indulgence, self-love, self-pity, self-pleasing, self-righteousness, self-seeking, self-sufficiency, self-trust, self-will.

Since God showed such love to overcome your predicament under God's anger, now, says John, you can luxuriate in God's love to you and let others relax in the knowledge of your love to them. Is there anything more challenging and searching in the entire Bible?

John has a further stage in his exposition, making the matter even more practical. **¹²No-one has seen God at any time. If we love one another God remains in us and His love is perfected in us**. One might tend to answer John: 'I do love God, I simply find it difficult to get on with so-and-so.' John exposes this as a pretext. It is too easy to claim to be getting on well with God. He is, after all, invisible. Our relationship with Him is a secret one, generally speaking. Easy claims about knowing God may cover up the very real battle we are having with loving people! John says, 'That brother or sister is right there in the fellowship. You see them every day. You can fool yourself that you love God, but it is not so easy to fool yourself that you love him or her!' If we *really* love God, we shall take steps to show love to our brothers and sisters. They are not 'spir-itual' and 'invisible' like God. They are solid flesh-and-blood. They are not far away. We begin by loving them.

If we do that, says John, 'God remains in us.' That is, we consciously enjoy His blessings in our lives. His in-dwelling presence becomes a reality. Others become aware that God is with us and in us.

Also 'His love is perfected in us'. It is as if love is with us 'in embryo', 'in a seed'. If we practise Christian love, the love of God within us becomes full-grown. God's love in our lives is brought to its intended full-measure when it flows through us to other people.

Maybe we are not very far along the pathway of love. John's challenge to us is that we venture forth today further down the road of love. It is the way God wants us to live. If we are born again we have the seed of love within us already.

Questions For Reflection: 1 John 4:7-12

1. How can we seek love without being sentimental and soft?
2. How do you measure love?
3. God is love. God is wrath. Are the two statements equally true?

21. God's Indwelling
1 John 4:13-16

John's great concern in his letter is that we might have fellowship with God. The Christian life, he has said, starts by our receiving the message of the apostles concerning Jesus. As soon as we receive the testimony concerning Jesus we begin to have what he calls 'fellowship with the Father and with the Son' (1:3, 6, 7). He also calls it 'knowing God' (2:3, 4). It is the enjoyment of being 'in Him' (2:5). It is 'abiding' or 'continuing' (2:24; 3:6) with the Father and the Son. Sometimes John describes this knowledge of God as a two-way 'continuing'. We 'continue' in fellowship with God and God 'continues' to impart His liveliness and His presence to us. God continues working in us and His love is perfected in us (4:12).

It is this two-way love relationship between the believer and God that is the theme of John's next paragraph.

(1) Dwelling in God is made a matter of conscious experience by the Holy Spirit. John says: **¹³By this we know that we remain in Him, and He remains in us: it is because He has granted us blessings from His Spirit**.

I have suggested before that in 1 John the verb 'know' (*ginosko*) does not refer to deductive logic but to conscious enjoyment of God's working in our lives in a way that we know about. There are expositors that virtually take the word here to mean to 'deduce' or 'prove', but there are objections to this approach.

The words 'By this we know' look forward to the reference to the Spirit at the end of the sentence. When John says we 'know' that we remain in Him, he is not referring

154

GOD'S INDWELLING   155

to persuading ourselves as a matter of logic or deduction
that we are continuing in God; he rather means that we are
consciously experiencing God. On another occasion, when
Paul asked, 'Did you receive the Spirit when you believed?'
(Acts 19:2), he was taking it for granted that they would
be able to give a clear yes/no answer. All over the New
Testament we find Christians who are *conscious* that they
have the Holy Spirit. They are aware of His leadings. His
presence is a foretaste of heaven. They are not 'deducing'
that they have the Spirit; they *know*!

John does not say precisely 'He has given us the Holy
Spirit'. What he says is, 'He has given us *from* the Holy
Spirit'. In other words, 'He has granted us blessings from
His Spirit'. The thought is similar to that of John 4:14
where the Holy Spirit is pictured as being an ever-flowing
spring within us giving us fresh and spontaneous supplies
every day.

'Whoever drinks of this water will thirst again,' said
Jesus to the Samaritan woman. This woman's life was a
drudge. She was obliged endlessly to be fetching her own
supply of water, which was exhausted almost as soon as
she had it. In contrast, said Jesus, the life of the Holy Spirit
which He gives us is a spring within us. There is no drudg-
ery; the source is a living, bubbling spring. The well of
Samaria required heavy lifting of buckets, reaching down
and pulling up. But a 'spring' bubbles up, bursts up under
its own pressure. This is John's picture of the Holy Spirit.
It is the Holy Spirit who imparts to us our remaining in
God, and God's remaining in us. The bi-directional
flowings of love and communication between God and us
take place by His working within us. On our side our
prayers to God are lifted aloft by the Spirit. On God's side

it is the Spirit who agitates and bubbles up within us. There
are His leadings, His promptings, His illuminations, His
encouragements, His empowerings, His impartation of
gifts. By the Spirit we dwell in God.

(2) The experience of God's indwelling is based upon the
historical facts of the gospel. There were people in Ephesus who were also speaking about knowing God. They
said in effect: 'Yes, John, we know about this dwelling in
God. God speaks to us and gives us elitist knowledge above
the common herd of humanity. We don't actually believe
that "the Christ" ever became flesh, but we know about
supernatural "knowledge" that gives us freedom from the
material "stuff" that this world is made of. We don't sin,
and ...'. But John will have nothing of any supposed
'knowledge of God' that bypasses the Son of God come
in the flesh. He adds: **14And we have seen and we bear witness that the Father sent the Son as the Saviour of the world**.

The point of verse 14 does not appear until one has
reached verses 15 and 16. The 'we' refers initially to the
apostles; then by faith and by the Spirit it refers to all
believers. John and his fellow apostles have seen and have
given witness concerning the *incarnate* Jesus. Those who
have experienced God are those who hold to the eyewitness testimony of the apostles. The apostles had fellowship with Jesus as those who had lived in literal and
physical contact with Him (see 1:1-3). After His ascen-
sion they experienced Jesus by the Spirit, but they knew
that the Jesus who gave them the Spirit was the Jesus whom
they had known on planet earth. Subsequent generations
must accept the eyewitness testimony of the apostles
before they will know the spiritual experience of dwelling

in God and having God dwell in them. So John says 'It is we, we apostles and those who believe our testimony, who have experience of God. No-one knows the *experience* of God who does not accept our apostolic message.'

John's words summarise the message:

(i) The Father and the Son were there before the time when Jesus came into the world ('...the Father sent the Son...').

(ii) Jesus was the incarnation of the divine Son ('And we have *seen* ... that the Father sent the Son...').

(iii) His mission in this world originated from God.

(iv) His work was a work of salvation ('...as the Saviour...').

(v) His work is available for all, not for a gnostic elite ('...the Saviour of the world').

(3) The experience of God's indwelling is based upon bold and openly confessed faith in the incarnate Son of God. We have seen John's point about the apostles, but what about the believers who come at a later stage of history? What about us? Later believers accept the apostolic testimony and boldly confess their faith in it. [15]**Anyone** – apostle, second-generation Christian, anyone! – **who confesses that Jesus is the Son of God, God remains in him and he remains in God**. The later generations of Christians believe in the apostolic testimony. They 'confess', that is, they publicly let everyone know that they have come to faith. Sooner or later, gradually or suddenly, they enter into the same experience of knowing God as the apostles had. The apostles had fellowship with the Father and the Son first; then we have it in and through the apostolic testimony. Only on this basis is the mutual indwelling of God and the believer experienced.

(4) The experience of God's indwelling brings great peace.
¹⁶And we have known and have relied on the love which God has among us. God is love, and he who abides in love abides in God, and God abides in him. This is one of the great heights of the Christian life: to *know* and to *trust* in God's love.

Knowing and to trusting in God's love involves *authority*. We 'know'. Like Charles Spurgeon we are able to say 'We have had access to Him in such a way we cannot have been deceived ... We were embraced of Him – no more at a distance.'[1] It is 'infallible assurance'.[2] 'We have known!' It is sharp clarity. It is illuminating light.

It involves *relying* or *confiding* in God's love. It is confidence in God's protection, confidence in God's provision, confidence in God's guidance, in His rescuings. It brings peace and joy. It brings a sense of direction.

It involves *a continuing love towards others*; it is the realisation that salvation is a kingdom of love! When you abide in God's love it not only brings you confidence and calmness and peace, it has to overflow to others also. If it does not overflow to others it will be lost to yourself. The fruit of the Spirit is love, joy, peace *in that order*. The outflowings of love to others bring inflowings of joy and peace to ourselves. It requires confiding in the love of God to be able to love others. It is very easy to talk and write about love, but every Christian knows what it is like when everything is against him. There are times when everything conspires to shatter our faith, but it is also true that every Christian experiences times when everything conspires to shatter his love.

1. C. H. Spurgeon, *Fellowship with God*, The New Park Street and Metropolitan Tabernacle Pulpit (1861, reprinted Pilgrim, 1973), p. 492.
2. *Westminster Confession of Faith*, ch. 18.

But we must go on; we must 'abide'. By continuing faith in the apostolic testimony, and by the regular day-by-day practice of Christian love we shall continue in God's love. If we love one another God remains in us. In practice this involves insisting on faith and insisting on love no matter what is happening to us. In trials, we believe and we show love. In delays, we believe and we show love. We walk in the Spirit. We resist legalism and harshness and needless severity. We admit what is happening to us.

This is perhaps the most vital practical sentence in this book: *to dwell in God's love involves insisting on faith and insisting on love no matter what is happening to us*. We have all failed at this point, but if we take John seriously we shall discover what Jesus meant: 'Whoever drinks from this water ... will never thirst again' (John 4:14).

Questions For Reflection: 1 John 4:13-16

1. What is it like to dwell in God?
2. Should we expect to feel God within us?
3. What is the difference between the 'spring' of the Spirit and the 'well' of the Spirit?

22. Love Perfected (part 1)
1 John 4:17-21

The apostle John is interested in bringing us to a high level of love. The early Methodists loved this section of 1 John and used to preach about 'perfect love'. In 1777, John Wesley wrote *A Plain Account of Christian Perfection*.[1] Sometimes they seemed to be teaching the very perfectionism that 1 John has repudiated, but they had *some* aspects of teaching from which we could learn. It is wonderful to be free from condemnation because we are clothed with the righteousness of Jesus Christ. But upon this foundation we need to be built up to high levels of love, boldness and graciousness. It is at this point where we need 1 John.

(1) There is such a thing as the love of God being 'perfected'. 1 John 4:17-18a reads: **By this is the love of God perfected, that we have boldness in the day of judgment, because as He is so also are we in this world. There is no fear in love**.

What is *perfected* love? Everyone who loves does so because he or she is born of God (4:7). In new birth a *capacity* for love is placed within us. The new Christian begins to love everyone. But this tends soon to be lost. We 'lose our first love' (Rev. 2:4). 'Un-perfected' love is love that has not yet become a determined principle, love that is knocked aside easily. When Christians show 'envy, strife and divisions' (1 Cor. 3:3), they show that their love has not yet been 'perfected'.

---

1. A cheap, unabridged, but slightly modernised version is *A Plain Man's Guide to Holiness* (Hodder, 1988).

'Perfected' love is not sinlessness! The early Methodists went wrong here. They were spiritual giants, and we could learn much from them. Their determination to reach 'perfect love' led them to be 'loud singers and shouters in their praises, long agonizers in their prayers, and lion-hearted laborers for their Lord'.[2] Their striving for the 'perfect love' led to enhancements in their lives. They *rightly* (to my mind) went beyond the Reformation tradition and looked for a higher level of holiness than most eighteenth-century Christians expected. They *rightly* (to my mind) broke with the idea that Romans 7:14-25 is 'normal Christianity'.[3] But they made some mistakes.

(i) They went too far in the way they used the word 'sinless' and in talking about the root of indwelling sinfulness being totally removed. Wesley said in 1767: 'I do not contend for the term *sinless*, though I do not object against it.'[4] His followers were less cautious. But once the term 'sinlessness' is introduced, problems start. Anyone who claims that sin is radically 'uprooted' has a dazzling reputation to live up to! It will only be a matter of time before sin gets redefined so that such are able to keep to the claim of sinlessness. This tends to lead into legalism and hypocrisy.

(ii) They spoke of such a blessing being immediately available by an act of instant, expectant, promise-claiming faith. From John Fletcher onwards they linked 'perfect love' with the baptism with the Spirit.

(iii) They had a rather confusing definition of sin as 'voluntary transgression of a known law', which enabled

2. J. I. Packer, *Keep In Step with the Spirit* (IVP, 1984), p. 133.
3. See my detailed exposition of this point in *Living Under Grace* (Nelson Word, 1994), chs. 26-50.
4. *Plain Man's Guide*, p. 122.

them to claim sinlessness and yet admit there were still *in*voluntary sins and sins against unknown requirements. It was sinlessness and yet it was not sinlessness.

(iv) The movement eventually split into two. When people look for an *experience* of sinlessness which does not come, they soon start 'claiming it by faith' without their having any 'experience'. The holiness movement divided into those who stressed 'experience' and those who stressed 'taking it by faith'. The latter was the 'Keswick' movement of the late nineteenth and early twentieth centuries. Instead of having 'experiences', they 'took' their blessings 'by faith'. Instead of 'eradication' of sin, they taught 'counteraction' of sinfulness (inbred sin is unchanged but thwarted by God's grace). Sometimes one half of the movement attacked the other half.[5]

People in revival may have such rich blessings that the claim to be without sin is simply the way they feel. But others who try to apply the teaching in their own lives get themselves into difficulties. Harry Ironside tried it and said:

> 'I searched my heart to see if I had made a full surrender and tried to give up every known thing that seemed in any sense evil or doubtful. Sometimes, for a month at a time, or even longer, I could persuade myself that at last I had received the blessing. But invariably a few weeks would bring before me once more that which *proved* that it was in my particular case all a delusion.'[6]

---

5. See A. M. Hills, *Scriptural Holiness and Keswick Teaching Compared* (Schmul, Ohio), n.d.
6. See H. Ironside, *Holiness the False and the True*, (Loizeaux, New Jersey, 1912, reprinted 1988), p. 23.

Christians whose experiences of the Spirit are not so dramatic, find that their sincere strivings and prayers for eradication of sin results in awful bondage.[7]

The Methodists were building on 1 John, but John is more clear-cut than they were. 'If we say we have no sin we are deceiving ourselves' (1:8). 'Perfected' love is not sinlessness! Rather it is love made into the determined principle of one's life. It is a habit of refusing to be judgmental. It is taking the initiative (as God in Jesus took the initiative) in bringing about reconciliation. It is the practice of total forgiveness without moralising the forgiven person. It is leaving vindication to God. It is practising the 'golden rule' of being sensitive to others (see Matt. 7:12). It is risking everything to be fearless in love. It is holding no grudges.

John actually speaks of *God's* love being perfected! By resting utterly in the love of God, by resting in the fact that God's anger has been propitiated, by knowing and utterly trusting in God's love for me, and *by turning this into a principle by which I love others*, the love of God is 'perfected'. It is brought to its intended fruition. We are never sinless; we need the blood of Jesus every day. But as long as we walk in the light we have peace of conscience for ourselves, graciousness towards others, boldness as those who live in God's presence, and (if Jesus comes) boldness to stand in His presence as forgiven sinners.

(2) The love of God is perfected in that 'we have boldness in the day of judgment'. John implies that not all Christians have boldness, and that lack of boldness is due to

---

7. The testimonies of Harry Ironside (*Holiness*, pp. 7-40), and J. I. Packer (*Keep In Step*, pp. 157-158) are painful but illuminating.

lack of love. This is true in this life and it will be true in the day of judgment. The second coming and the day of resurrection will be a day of reward (see Rev. 22:12). Although every Christian will be covered with the righteousness of Jesus in the judgment, and that will be his only hope of heaven, yet it does not mean that every Christian will be equally confident.

It might seem to be impossible to be bold amidst judgment if we are to be judged by our works (see 2 Cor. 5:10). Yet there is a way. When the Christian walks in love, his conscience is cleansed (see 1:7). Such a one is not perfect, but he is *cleansed*. If he knew Jesus were to come in a few minutes time it would make no difference. He has assured fellowship with God now. Not every Christian has this. Not every Christian will be without shame at the second coming of Jesus. The way to know such boldness is to walk in love.

(3) John assures us of the possibility of perfected love because of the resources of the heavenly Jesus. The love of God is perfected, and we have boldness in the day of judgment, *because as He is so also are we in this world*.

What is the precise point of the added remark, 'because as He is so also are we in this world'? One must note that it does not say 'as He was', but 'as He is'. Right now, at this very moment, Jesus is at the right hand of the Father. According to what He is – right now at this moment – so are we in this world. It means that our position in this world is determined by what Jesus is now, as He is at the right hand of the Father.

We must follow the trend of thought in what John has just said. He is urging us to reach to great heights of love, but (we ask) is it really possible? Is it possible to have a clear conscience? Is it possible to know that although one is never sinless, yet one can be so totally cleansed in conscience as to be bold before God now and bold before God on judgement day? John answers: Yes! As He is so also are we in this world! We now live on earth in accordance to what He is in heaven! He is there ready to pour down upon us the supplies of the Spirit. He is Lord of our every situation. He constantly presents our needs before the Father.

Can we live the life of love? Yes! According to what He is in glory, according to a heavenly Advocate who is able to do far more abundantly above all that we ask or even think, according to His heavenly power that is at work in our earthly situation, according to His power that is at work in us – so are we in this world.

Can we live the life of love? Yes!

Can we walk with cleansed consciences? Yes!

Can we hope to be bold in the day of judgment? Yes!

Questions For Reflection: 1 John 4:17-21

1. 'Building up high levels of love.' How might we do this?
2. A 'higher level of holiness'? What do you think of this? Have Christians in days gone by been too complacent?
3. How can sin get 'redefined'?

23. Love Perfected (part 2)
1 John 4:17-21

We have seen: (1) There is such a thing as the love of God being 'perfected'; (2) Love, when perfected, gives 'boldness in the day of judgement'; and (3) perfected love is possible because of the resources of the heavenly Jesus. But John has yet more to say.

(4) John goes on to portray love. Essentially it is freedom from fear. The end of verse 17 says: **There is no fear in love**. Verse 18 belongs with verse 17. **But this perfect love throws out fear, because fear holds on to punishment, and he who fears is not perfected in love.**

Why are we unloving? John says it is because we are afraid, afraid about ourselves, our security, our pleasure, our reputation, our future. We are unloving because we are defensive and self-protective. Supremely, we are afraid of punishment, punishment from God *now*, punishment from God when judgment finally comes. We are afraid of some kind of punishment from other people. We have a fear that they will not like us, that they will reject us, oppose us, criticize us. The root of being unloving is always fear, and always fear of punishment.

But love is the opposite of all of this. Fear and love are opposites. Fear and faith are opposites. Faith and love are companions.

'This perfect love throws out fear.' One characteristic of John's style is that many phrases can be taken in several ways and yet each way seems valid. The multiple ambiguity that irritates Brown and is seen as a defect[1] is

---

1. Brown, *Epistles*, page x.

possibly an indication of the richness of John's deceptively simple language.

Thus the meaning here could be (i) our love (or God's love) throws out our fear of the other person, or (ii) our love (or God's love) throws out the fear that the other person has for us, (iii) our love (or God's love) throws out the terror we would have of God because of our feelings of guilt and (iv) – if the repercussions continue – *our* love will cast out *the other person's* sense of terror before God and make him or her feel forgiven, accepted and reassured. John says in effect: take it whichever way you like. The kingdom of God is an entire realm of love. At every point it is a fear-removing regime. At every point and in half-a-dozen ways it banishes every kind of intimidation.

John goes deeper still: **fear holds on to punishment**. The deepest aspect of fear is that it is fear of punishment. We feel guilty and almost expect to be punished. We feel angry and find within us the kind of resentment which (if we have any insight into ourselves) we see as a desire to punish.

But 'this perfect love throws out fear, because fear holds on to punishment' and perfect love wants nothing to do with either fear or punishment.

'Perfect love' has as its deepest base the conviction that God loves us. It begins with the assurance that *we* ourselves do not need to have any fear of this kind because punishment has been turned aside from us. Even if we sin, we have an Advocate, and He is the propitiation for our sins. Punishment has been averted.

> I will praise You, O LORD,
>   Although You were angry with me,
> Your anger has certainly turned away
>   and You have comforted me (Isa. 12:1).

We are reconciled to God, not just because we are willing to have Him, but because He is satisfied with the blood
of His Son, and is eager to have us. We can 'know God's
love'; we can trust utterly in His determination to keep us
and care for us.

'Perfect love' is when this conviction that God loves us
becomes the base on which we treat others. 'Perfect love'
is when we live in a way that is 'throwing out' every kind
of fear of punishment. It is when we *insist* on loving others, despite the opposition of the devil and lurking animosities within our own hearts. It is when we refuse to
allow the other person to fear us. It is when we have confidence in God's love towards us and are eager to bring
others into confidence that God loves them. In half-a-dozen
ways perfect love 'throws out fear' and refuses to live in
an atmosphere of punishment.

He who fears is not perfected in love (4:18). There are
people – sometimes we are among them – who fall into
unloving ways. Even in the church of Jesus there can be
criticism, quiet complaining, gossiping, rivalry. John's
analysis of us when we are like that is not that we do not
understand doctrine, not that we have the wrong temperament, not that circumstances are very difficult for us, but
that we are not perfected in love. At bottom we have not
really seen how much God loves us. When we are made
complete in God's love to us, it will be easier for us to be
renewed in love.

(5) John develops the point that the kind of love he has in
mind depends on love received by ourselves. **[19]We love
because He first loved us** (The Authorised Version, 'We

love him', is a mistake[2]). To lose ourselves in the love of
God is the way to get to love others. Lovelessness towards
others is rooted in insecurity. If we felt loved, we would
show love. Verse 19 is also a rebuke to incipient pride.
'Perfect love' is a high level of godly living. Where would
be the humility of the Christian who claimed it? John's
words are a counterbalance to self-righteousness. If the
Christian *does* show love it is because behind human love
is God's prior love. Any love that anyone ever shows is
generated by the love of God in Jesus.

That this view of verse 19 is correct is made more probable by the continuation in verse 20 which goes on to deal
with the person's claim ('If anyone says...'). The claim to
love for God is to be validated by brotherly love (verse 20).

(6) Love of God's people is essential to love of God. **[20]If
anyone says I love God and yet he hates his brother, he is a
liar. For the one who does not love his brother or sister whom
he has seen, cannot be loving God whom he has not seen**.
The point here is not that love of God is more difficult
than love of people. It is not, 'If you do not do the easier
thing, how can you be doing the more difficult thing?'
Rather the point is that love of people is more *tangible*,
more *obvious*, more *observable* by others. A person might
say 'I love God'. Who can prove whether he does or
whether he does not? Yet if the same person says 'I love
people', the evidence is nearer to hand! God is Spirit. To
love Him might seem very 'spiritual', very 'devotional'.
It might seem to be largely a matter of prayers and singing
and attending meetings. 'I love God!' we might say, but

---

2. There is a textual variant here and the Authorised Version was following inferior manuscripts.

then God cannot be seen and our love is expressing itself
mainly in acts of worshipful devotion. There is something
more tangible about loving people! We cannot fool ourselves quite so easily when it comes to loving people. The
criterion of loving God is not what we feel in worship, it is
what we feel when we are with our brother, who is a tangible reality.

(7) John asks us to accept this as an obligation that God
lays upon us. As often in 1 John a statement (verse 20)
becomes a command (verse 21). **²¹And this is the command
we have from Him, that he that loves God should love his
brother also**. We need to lose ourselves in the love of God,
and then cultivate a sweetness of spirit towards others. We
need to make it the principle of our lives to refuse
ungodly talk about others, to reject bitterness and lasting
wrathfulness, to restrain harsh and rough speaking. One
wonders how John himself came to such love. There was a
time when he was known as a 'son of thunder' (Mark 3:17).
But God is able to deal with us! He knows how to make
just the right mixture of circumstances that will rebuke us
and train us. The 'son of thunder' is sweetly pressurised
into becoming the 'apostle of love'.

How do we cultivate such love? When we simply make
resolutions ('I promise not to lose my temper ... not to get
angry ... not to complain ...'), we shall probably break them
the same day as we make them. A better way is to begin
with God's love to us. Then we had best be honest about
ourselves. Perhaps we are lacking in patience or in gentleness. Perhaps we have proud ways or inconsiderateness.
Perhaps we exaggerate or twist the truth. We had best
humble ourselves before God, admit the way things are

with us, and accept the fact that we are still accepted by
God because of the blood of Jesus.

There is something very crushing about accepting the
truth about ourselves and yet knowing that God still
accepts us. It somehow enables us to leave our case and
our cause in the hands of God. We become like Jesus. We
surrender our reputation, our conviction that we are right,
our passionate desires to have things our own way. And
we accept the fact that there is something far more important, 'the command we have from Him'.

Questions For Reflection: 1 John 4:17-21

1. 'Perfect love throws out fear.' Are you truly fearless?
2. Are we unloving because we are afraid?
3. Is it good to take Scriptural phrases in many ways?

24. Faith, Love, Overcoming
1 John 5:1-5

(1) In his quest to produce a loving company of followers, John starts this section by defining what he means by a brother or sister. He begins: **¹Everyone who believes that Jesus is the Christ has been begotten of God**.

New birth is the cause of faith. There are five other times in 1 John where he directly puts to us the results of new birth. (i) New birth produces righteousness (2:29). (ii) New birth prevents easy sinning (3:9). (iii) New birth produces love (4:7). (iv) New birth overcomes the world (5:4). (v) New birth gives us protection from Satan (5:18).

One might think that 1 John 5:1 is saying 'Faith causes new birth'. However, the parallel statements and the tenses that he uses ('Everyone who believes ... has been begotten ...') make it clear that the point is the other way round. To the five results of new birth mentioned elsewhere we must add a sixth: (vi) new birth is the source of faith (5:1).

Faith is evidence that a person is born of God. Often the New Testament puts it the other way round, and says that it is faith that leads to the gift of the Spirit, and the gift of the Spirit is the evidence of faith (which is the point of Acts 10:45-47). 'Asking' leads to 'drinking' Jesus' living water (John 4:10). Believing leads to the end of thirst (John 6:35; 7:37-39). Repentance and faith expressed in baptism lead to the promised gift of the Spirit (Acts 2:38). The Spirit is given to those who obey God in faith (Acts 5:32). The Spirit fell on those who believed (Acts 10: 43,44); the gift of the Spirit seals faith (Acts 11:14; Gal. 3:2; Acts 19:2; Eph. 1:13). These are references to the 'sealing' of the Spirit.

There is a second group of Scripture-passages which do not seem to be quite identical to the ones just mentioned, but which still refer to a new life which comes as the result of faith. It is faith that justifies and it is the justified person who receives 'life' (Rom. 5:12-21). In this group would come such Scriptures as 1 Peter 1:23 and James 1:18. In John 3:36 it is those who believe on the Son that have life, not 'those who have life believe'. In John 20:21 it is not that 'having life, we believe' but 'believing, we have life'.

Then, there are Scriptures that refer to an even earlier and deeper work of the Spirit. There has to be a work of the Spirit before there can be faith. No one can call Jesus 'Lord' except by the Spirit (1 Cor. 12:3). The natural man cannot receive the things of the Spirit of God (1 Cor. 2:14). No-one can come to Jesus except by the drawing of the Father (John 6:44). 1 John 5:1 is similar. In its deepest origins faith is a gift of God, the result of the quickening work of the Spirit. John goes *behind* faith. How does it come about that a person ever believes in Jesus? John shares with us something which (like the doctrine of election) is a family secret. Although we do not realise it at the time, behind our faith is the quickening, enlivening and secret work of the Holy Spirit bringing us to new birth. John Stott is right: 'believing is the consequence, not the cause, of the new birth'.[1]

(2) Secondly, John goes on to say **and everyone who loves the One who does the begetting also loves the one who is born of God** (5:1b). Or, as the New International Version puts it, *and everyone who loves the Father loves his child.*

---

1. Stott, *Epistles*, p. 172.

New birth imparts something of the character of God within us. In new birth, God puts new desires within us, a new frame of mind, a magnetic attraction towards God and His pure and holy ways. The Father, 'the one who does the begetting', imparts this life to every one of His children. God's aim is to produce a family of love. If 'the one who begets' imparts His own holy character to each of His children, it is to be expected that whatever differences might be among them because of their earthly origins (nationality, tribe, class, temperament, education, status, skin colour, level of wealth), will be over-ridden by what they have in common, the nature of God within them. If we are born of God and have the capacity and inclination to love the Father, the same new birth and the same love of God's character will lead us to love the Father's children. The new birth produces both kinds of love, which at root is only one kind of love.

(3) John's next concern is that the love he is urging should be rightly understood. He says, **²By this we know that we love the children of God, when we love God and do His commands**. At first this verse might seem to put things the wrong way round. After everything John has written so far, we expect him to say 'we know that we love God, when we love the children of God and obey God's commands'.

It is true both ways round. Real love for God is shown by love of His children, but it is also true that love of His children is authentic only when it arises from love for God, and the particular ways in which He demands we show love: His 'commands'. Not every kind of benevolence is really the kind of love John is talking about. Even less is the world's licentious expression of its sexuality worthy of being called 'love'. Love is the test of knowledge of God, but knowledge of God is also the test of love.

(4) Next, John speaks of the ease of keeping the commands of love. **³For this is the love of God, that we keep His commands and His commands are not burdensome**. John's ability to surprise us is endless. We might not be ready to think that the commands of love are 'not burdensome'.

Love is definable: it has commands, it has content. It is not rightly expressed in the *Mosaic* law, and legislation is always inadequate to articulate what it means to love. But this does not mean that love cannot be expressed in words at all. The New Testament is full of exhortations which are partial expressions of the love-command. Although no list of commands can encapsulate every requirement for every situation, yet each practical exhortation of the New Testament is a twinkling flash of light from the sparkling diamond of the love-command. John does not give a list of requirements. It would be casuistry to do so, the promotion of a law-code, a list of demands which when kept is thought to be love.

It is quite possible to produce details of the love-command when required to do so, as the New Testament shows with its richness of precise exhortations. The one-and-only love-command will require prayer for one's enemies, endurance under ill-treatment, practical action when need is evident, and so on. These are 'His commands', but they cannot be entirely encapsulated in a list. A list of ten commandments or ten thousand commandments would still not convey what is meant by love, and what it means to 'walk in the Spirit'. John and Paul (Rom. 13:8-10) like to think of *one* command, although they can think of many

commands. They were following in the steps of Jesus
(Matt. 7:12).

Is God's will not sometimes burdensome? The New
Testament surprises us by insisting that it is not! Jesus'
yoke is easy; his burden is light (Matt. 11:30). This might
perplex us because most Christians have known times
when the will of God has been agonizingly painful, and
they have shrunk from some high demand put upon them.

The answer to our perplexity comes in our *experience*
of yielding to God. The will of God seems agonizingly
difficult ahead of our obedience to it, but when we actually get to doing His will it turns out to be light after all!
He carries the load. There is such a supply of grace. His
burden is indeed light. His yoke is indeed easy! We shall
never discover this fact unless we discover it in experience. When we yield to Him in body and in mind we *prove*
in experience that His will is 'good, acceptable and perfect' (Rom. 12:1-2).

(5) Who can love in such a way? 1 John 5:4 answers: we
can! John says God's commands are not burdensome, **'For
everyone born of God overcomes the world. And this is the
victory that overcame the world, it is our faith**. He then
goes on to define the content of that faith. **⁵And who is the
one who overcomes the world other than the one who believes that Jesus is the Son of God**. Verse 4 explains ('For
...') why the commands of God are not burdensome. It is
because of the Christian's spiritual birth and his persistent
faith. The movement of thought from verses 1-3 to verse 4
shows that the 'world' are those characterised by deficiency
in faith (verse 1) and a deficient love (verses 2-3). The
present tense, 'overcomes', points to the permanent pos-

sibility of overcoming the world; the simple past (or
'aorist') tense of 'overcame' points to the recent victory
the followers of John have experienced. The departure of
John's enemies has been the result of persistent faith on
the part of John's disciples.[2] In verse 5 John changes back
to a present tense. The faith that has recently won a victory may do so constantly. John points to what it means to
love. It is to persist in faith no matter what is happening to
us. Then we conquer the world; we conquer lovelessness.

Questions For Reflection: 1 John 5:1-5

1. The Spirit works faith in us. Faith brings the Spirit. Can
you think of Scriptures that teach both these truths?
2. How can we know whether we really are showing love?
3. Can love be defined without laws?

---

2. For this view over against the idea that it is the victory that Christ has
won (Westcott) or the conversion of the disciples of John, see Stott, *Epistles*, p. 174.

25. The Testimony to the Gospel (part 1)
1 John 5:6-12

We have seen how faith overcomes the world and its love-lessness. But it must not be thought that it is *any* kind of 'faith' that John has in mind. What John has in mind is faith in Jesus the Son of God come in the flesh. Now he puts before us a paragraph which emphasizes in a most forceful way the reality of Jesus' coming into this world as a man.

(1) Jesus comes to us in three ways. **⁶This is the one who came through water and blood, Jesus Christ. He did not come by water only, but by water and by blood. And the Spirit is the one who witnesses because the Spirit is the truth.**

The word 'came' apparently means not just 'came into this world', but 'came into the position of being a Saviour, came to us through certain historical events which enable Him to give us eternal life'. There were circumstances and events 'through' which Jesus 'came' in order to reach us as a Saviour.

He came *through water*. He was there before His baptism as the Son of God. But His ministry to us involved His 'coming' to us through water. He was Son of God before His baptism, but the baptism was the occasion of His being empowered by the Holy Spirit.

He came *through blood*. That is to say, He had to die, and His death was real. John has already said that it is the blood of Jesus that turned aside the Father's anger against sin (2:2; 4:10). It is the blood of Jesus that cleanses the conscience of the Christian who 'walks in the light' (1:7). The historical fact that Jesus, the Son of God, died upon the cross for us is indispensable to His 'coming' to us.

The words 'He did not come by water only, but by water and by blood' must allude to those false teachers who maintained that 'the Christ' came down upon Jesus at His baptism, but left Jesus before His death, so that 'the Christ' did not truly die. The precise identity of those who taught this is not absolutely clear. It is likely that there was *more* than one gnostic group in Ephesus. Certainly the heretic Cerinthus lived in Ephesus and he taught that the heavenly Christ came upon Jesus at His baptism, but left Him before His death.

Such ideas were certainly circulating in John's area. Such a notion regards 'Jesus' and 'the Christ' as two distinct personalities. 'Jesus' died (on this view) but 'Jesus Christ the Son of God' did not. John will have none of this. 'Jesus Christ ... did not come by water only, but by water and by blood.' That is, the man Jesus was also the Christ, the Son of God. He became a true man. He 'came' to us by being empowered at his baptism. He 'came' to us by truly dying upon the cross.

The Spirit's witness is needed also. The tense used in connection with the first two items is a past tense: 'the one who *came* through water and blood'. But now John must use a present tense: 'the Spirit *is* the one who witnesses'. The historical events of baptism and death were vital, but they were not enough. Jesus finally 'comes' to us through the witness of the Spirit. The Spirit is the one who witnesses, because the Spirit is the truth.

All of these things had to take place. Jesus could not have helped us had it not been for the power of the Spirit which came upon Him at His baptism. He could not have helped us had He not died for us. But there has to be a

third ingredient. Jesus ministers to us by the Spirit's
witness.

When the Spirit is at work He glorifies Jesus. He adds
His testimony to the historical facts. The Spirit will not
work in power where the full teaching concerning Jesus
as the Son of God is not upheld. No authentic 'outpouring' of the Spirit ever falls upon destructive heresy. What
happened on the occasion mentioned in Acts 10:44 will
not and does not take place where a false Christ is com-
municated. Peter was preaching about Jesus as 'Lord of
all' (Acts 10:36). He mentioned his authentic humanity
('Jesus of Nazareth') and Jesus' empowerment by the Spirit
at His baptism (Acts 10:38), His death upon the cross (Acts
10:39) and the reality of His humanity even after His
resurrection from the dead (Acts 10:41). Peter put before
them *this* Jesus as the object of faith (Acts 10:43). And
the Holy Spirit 'fell on' those who were listening with
faith in their hearts (Acts 10:44). The Spirit is the one
who witnesses because the Spirit is the truth. He will not
witness to anything else.

(2) John's next point is that these three events witness to
the nature of Jesus as the Son of God. Verse 7 says: *For
there are three that testify,...* and verse 8 continues, *the
Spirit and the water and the blood, and the three are in
agreement.* There are some famous extra words in the
Authorised Version of 1 John 5:7, 'There are three that
bear record in heaven, the Father, the Word, and the Holy
Ghost ...' but these words are not in any *respected* Greek
manuscript at all! They were taken from a Latin composi-
tion (not a biblical text) by a fourth century Spanish Christian, and were then inserted into the Latin New Testament

manuscripts. In about AD 800 it became part of the Vulgate, the official Latin Bible of the medieval church. Later still, after the fourteenth century, the words were translated from Latin to Greek and were included in a few inferior Greek manuscripts. Erasmus, who first published a printed Greek New Testament, was forced against his will, by his enemies, to include them in his third edition of the Greek New Testament, and so they got into the text which was used by the translators of the Authorised Version. They are certainly not original. The doctrine of the Trinity does not depend on this verse alone. The extra words should be ignored by readers of the Authorised Version.

John says: **⁸There are three that testify, the Spirit and the water and the blood ...**

The Spirit testifies. He does so externally and He continues to do so internally. Externally the giving of the Spirit is sometimes so vibrant an experience that it becomes visible to onlookers. When Jesus received the Spirit, John the Baptist saw something (John 1:32). On the day of Pentecost the events of the outpouring of the Spirit were externally visible and audible (Acts 2:3) and the experience was also visible and audible to those who saw the disciples. They spoke in tongues (Acts 2:4), and within no time at all a crowd of thousands had gathered. The *message* that was proclaimed on that occasion was about 'Jesus of Nazareth ... a man ...' (Acts 2:22). Peter went on to describe Him as God's Messiah who had truly died (Acts 2:23). He is, said Peter, 'the Lord' (Acts 2:25). God had made Him 'Lord and Christ' (2:36). The Spirit's being poured out was testimony to the faith of the hundred and twenty disciples who believed that Jesus was the Son of God come in the flesh. It sealed their faith and empowered the further preaching of that faith. Later in the book of Acts there were further outpourings of the Spirit (Acts 8:14-17; 10:34-48; 19:1-7). They were always confirmations of the message that Jesus is the Son of God come in the flesh.

The Spirit also testifies internally and invisibly. The main thing the Holy Spirit does in our hearts is testify to Christ. He is a secret inward Teacher. He illumines, convicts and persuades. The message He writes upon our hearts is a message concerning our own sinfulness and concerning the life that is to be found in Jesus Christ, the Son of God.

The Spirit's testimony is not simply an inward experience with no attestation outside of ourselves. The Spirit's testimony is an application of the testimony of previous historical events.

The water testifies. At the time of Jesus' baptism the voice from heaven attested to Jesus' Sonship ('You are my Beloved Son') and His obedience ('In you I am well pleased'). John the Baptist actually saw a visible manifestation of the Holy Spirit (John 1:32) and as a result testified, 'This is the Son of God' (John 1:34).

The blood testifies. At the cross of Jesus there were eyewitnesses who saw Him shed His blood. Although the 'water' of 1 John 5, and the 'water' of John 19:34 are not the same and the similarity between the two passages is a coincidence, yet the reference to blood there illuminates our passage. The soldier saw the blood and 'has given testimony, and his testimony is true. He knows that he tells the truth, and he testifies ... These things happened ...' (John 19:35-36).

Although these three witnesses are different kinds of witness, yet 'the three are in agreement'. It was an Old Testament legal principle that in any court case no evidence was to be accepted unless the witnesses agreed. John applies that legal maxim. The witness of history and the witness of the Spirit testify to the same thing: Jesus is the Son of God in the flesh. What happened in history and what happens in our hearts comes together. The gospel message begins outside of us. It is an announcement, 'good news', of what God has done. But something has to happen inside our hearts as well. There is no gospel without the historical events. There is no salvation without the inward conviction that the events are true and to be trusted. It is this faith, brought about by the Holy Spirit, that overcomes the world and its lovelessness.

Questions For Reflection: 1 John 5:6-12

1. How important was the baptism of Jesus?
2. What is important: facts of history or facts of experience?
3. Is Christian faith dependent on historical certainty?

26. The Testimony to the Gospel (part 2)
1 John 5:6-12

The faith that John regards as authentic is one that holds to certain historical facts. 'Water' and 'blood' refer to two historical events which John insists actually took place in the life of Jesus the Son of God. It is to these historical events that the Spirit bears witness, that is, He brings persuasion in the human heart. The Spirit's witness and the witness of the historical events cohere (5:8).

(1) The Christian takes notice of 'witnesses' to the historical events (5:9). John says **⁹If we receive human testimony the testimony of God is greater. For this is the testimony of God which He has testified concerning His Son**. The gospel involves human testimony. The apostles insisted on some historical events which they personally witnessed. There was a generation of apostles who made emphatic claims about the events in which they were involved. Luke wrote his gospel while keeping in touch with those who were 'eyewitnesses' (Luke 1:2). John's Gospel was written by one who claimed to be 'bearing witness to these things' (John 21:24). Paul claimed special authority because he had met with Jesus personally: 'Have I not *seen* Jesus our Lord?' he would ask (1 Cor. 9:1). Peter could insist that he personally had seen the glory of Christ when he went with Jesus at the time of His transfiguration: 'We were eyewitnesses of His majesty ... we heard His voice ... we were with Him' (2 Peter 1:18).

The Christian faith is rooted in history. There is no fellowship with God unless Jesus' claims for Himself are accepted. 'The testimony of God is greater', but the human testimony of the apostles also has importance.

(2) Yet there is another side to the matter. The human witness of the apostles to the facts of the gospel is of vital importance, yet *the agency that finally secures faith is the Spirit*. 'If we receive human testimony' (which we do!) 'the testimony of God is greater.'

From the time of the 'Enlightenment' in Europe (about 1680s to 1750s) it has been customary to disparage the trustworthiness of history. The 'human testimony' of men concerning historical facts has often seemed to be a flimsy and unreliable thing. Gotthold Lessing (1729-1781) started a mood of doubt about history by speaking disparagingly of 'accidental truths of history' and said it was not possible to get across the 'ugly broad ditch' from history to truth. From that day onwards Christian scholars have been bothered about 'Lessing's ugly ditch'.

John's reply to that difficulty would be: 'If we receive human testimony, the testimony of God is greater.' The facts of the gospel are there for anyone to investigate, yet over and above the human testimony is the testimony of the Holy Spirit.

This is not to play down the historical facts. John maintains that they are vital. John has made it quite clear that for him Jesus is a real figure of history. It was possible to see Him, hear Him, gaze upon Him, touch Him. He was baptized; He received the Spirit; He died. He is now the 'message of life' at the right hand of the Father. This is all thoroughly tangible and factual.

Yet the thing that brings certainty and assurance is the working of the Holy Spirit. 'The testimony of God is

greater!' It is greater than human testimony, because of its
greater certainty, its greater power to convince, its greater
reliability. This working of the Holy Spirit is very personal. The Holy Spirit presses upon our hearts what He
knows to be true. His convicting can be powerful. We
simply know that something is true. The veil over the truth
is taken away. The veil of blindness over our own hearts is
also taken away, and we see the truth with clarity and conviction. This is greater than historical argumentation, and
it is the way in which we get to be utterly sure that the
historical claims are true.

(3) John is not speaking of a vague experience. The message of the gospel has definite content to it. It is 'concerning His Son'. The reality of the fact that Jesus is the Son
of God in the flesh is the message to which the Spirit will
give His attestation.

(4) It follows, says John, that the Christian will be a person of assurance and conviction. The believer possesses
the indwelling Spirit and thus has certainty that the witness to the gospel that he has heard is true: **¹⁰The one who
believes in the Son of God has the testimony in himself.** This
is a further difference between human testimony and the
testimony of the Spirit. Human testimony is external. It
consists of historical witnesses and evidences of one kind
or another. Human testimony may be forgotten, becoming
lost in antiquity. But the testimony of the Spirit is a testimony within. When a person becomes a Christian the Spirit
is given to dwell within him. From that point on he 'has
the testimony in himself'. It is something that he or she is
conscious of. Obviously! What would be the value of a

witness that we did not know about? It gives us joy. We find delight in our salvation springing up within us. It gives assurance and boldness. It gives us love for God, because the witness of the Spirit makes us realise how much God loves us. It has the effect of stirring up our love for God. We can endure almost anything, make any sacrifice, if the witness of the Spirit is strong and powerful in our lives. The witness of the Spirit makes God real to us. When the Spirit is witnessing that we are children of God it is like being in heaven already.

(5) It follows then that to resist the claims of the Lord Jesus Christ is in effect to call God a liar. Unbelief is a sin against God's testimony. **The one who does not believe God has made Him a liar, because he has not believed in the testimony which God has testified concerning His Son** (5:10b). God asks us to believe the revelation He has already given. He has no plans to add anything further to convince us. He wants us to be convinced by His Word, coming to us in the testimony of the apostles.

This way of thinking about the matter helps us to see that there can be no neutrality concerning faith or unbelief. No-one can adopt a neutral position. If one is not trusting Jesus as the Son of God, one is in effect calling God a liar. God has testified. The voice came from heaven at Jesus' baptism. Eyewitnesses tell us they saw Him shedding His blood. Some tell us they were eyewitnesses of His majesty. The day of Pentecost came, and two thousand years of church history have followed with endless accounts of the power of salvation in the lives of men and women. God will give no further proofs. He has said all He has to say about His Son. No fuller revelation

about Jesus will come until Jesus Himself comes. The
question now is simply, will we believe what God has said
or will we call Him a liar?

(6) Within our hearts, the testimony brings life. **¹¹And this
is the testimony: God gave us eternal life, and this life is in
His Son**. This speaks of the two sides of the witness of the
Spirit. Within, the Spirit gives us assurance that we have
eternal life; but such a witness is built upon the foundation that such eternal life is in the historically manifested
Son of God. The essence of the Christian gospel is life.
What happens when a person receives Jesus Christ by faith
in the testimony of the apostles is that he comes alive. The
Christian is a person who has been made alive with a life
that comes from God's Son. It is a life which is full of
sensitivity to God and His Spirit. It is energy, liveliness, a
desire to do things for God. It is understanding and clarity. When others are fuzzy and confused about the things
of God, for the Christian the gospel is self-evident and
plain. He is no longer dead to the things of God; he is
alive to them. 'Eternal life' is clarity concerning God in
the mind; appetite for God in the desires; capacity to obey
God within our willpower. And it goes on and on; it grows
and develops. Eternal life is a growing life, an ever-
increasing life.

John wants to put this as sharply as he can. **¹²He who
has the Son has life. He who does not have the Son of God
does not have life**. It is a simple either/or matter. The experience of eternal life is altogether a matter of having the
Son of God or not having Him. At this point the entire
human race divides into two groups. Eternal life is in
Jesus alone. If you do not have Jesus you do not have any

liveliness towards God. Without Jesus there is no hope of heaven, no hope of glory beyond the grave. 'Eternal life' is the life of eternity, the life of heavenly glory, but we do not have to wait until after the grave to get it! Anyone who has Jesus has this 'life of eternity' already. It is a foretaste of heaven. It is the energy of heaven, the praise of heaven, the joy of God's presence which will characterise heaven. We have it now, if we have Jesus, and it will grow and grow, 'shining more and more unto the perfect day' (Prov. 4:18, AV).

Questions For Reflection: 1 John 5:6-12

1. Is Christian faith dependent on historical certainty?
2. Is there such a thing as sincere doubt?
3. How would you counsel a person who says he wants proof of the gospel?

27. Knowing Eternal Life
1 John 5:13-17

The situation in Ephesus to which John was writing was painful. Obviously the churches had been through a time of conflict. John is coming towards the end of his letter of encouragement and clarification. One of his final encouragements is to remind them that they can pray! Beyond this there are a number of things that John wants for the believers.

(1) He wants them to have a fresh experience of eternal life: **¹³I write these things to you, you who believe in the name of the Son of God, in order that you might know that you have eternal life**.

It is worth noting how much John wants these people to regain a consciousness of eternal life within them. He wants them to know that their gnostic enemies know nothing of salvation. It is a terrible thing when doubts about the person of Jesus have robbed a Christian of the lively flowings of the Holy Spirit within him. It is terrible to be uncertain when there is no need to be so. John knows these people. He knows they have believed in the gospel of Jesus and so he feels quite confident about giving them his personal word of assurance. Zane Hodges is right to point out that 'these things' does not refer to the whole letter, but to the things John has just said (just as similar phrases in 2:1, 26 refer to what immediately precedes).[1] John's point is that if they rest directly on the testimony of God about Jesus they will experience the flowing of eternal

---

Z. Hodges, '1 John' in *The Bible Knowledge Commentary: New Testament* (Victor, 1984), p. 902.

life within them. Assurance will bring joy and vibrancy to their lives. Assurance may be confirmed by the simple things he has put before them in 5:6-12.

He writes not (be it noted) that they may decide *whether or not* they have eternal life. Rather John writes to reassure them that they *do* have eternal life. John feels sure about them. His affirmation is wholly positive at this point. He has given them a restatement of the nature of the gospel in such a way that they may be sure that it is they – and not John's enemies – who stand in the tradition of authentic faith.

It might be asked: did these Christians not have assurance of salvation already? To which it may be said that the experience of eternal life welling up within them is more than 'assurance of salvation', and secondly that the Christians of Ephesus had obviously been unsettled by their experience with the gnostic heretics and needed John's word of encouragement.

(2) John also wants them to pray: **¹⁴And this is the confidence that we have towards Him, that if we ask anything according to His will, He hears us**. One reason why it is vital they know they are experiencing eternal life is that it will affect their praying. If we know that we believe, if we know that we are praying in His will, then we may also know that the answer to that prayer is on its way. John does say 'if'. Sometimes we do not have a 100% assurance that what we are praying for is God's will. God allows us to pray generally. But if in our relationship to Him we come to know that we are praying in His will, a wonderful confidence in prayer follows. **¹⁵And if we know that He hears us in whatever we ask, we know that we have**

the requests that we have asked from Him. Again we note
that John does say 'if'. Sometimes we pray and we do not
know that He hears us. But we can still pray! And God
may answer us even if we do not have total certainty that
what we are asking for is His will. But if we *do* know He
hears us, we have it! It may be slow in coming, slow in
being visibly realised, but the actual answer to the prayer
has already been approved. To have this kind of knowledge in advance gives great peace and joy.

(3) The controversial situation in Ephesus has been so
fierce John must tell them to pray for those who are struggling with doubts concerning the false teachers. Some of
John's friends have fallen into lovelessness and neglect of
the Christian brotherhood. But the Christians can help each
other. **[16]If anyone sees his brother or sister sinning a sin which
does not lead to death, he will pray and he shall give him life,
for those who sin but whose sin does not lead to death**. The
'he' ... 'he' ... 'him' may be interpreted variously. Is it that
the Christian shall pray and *God* will give the fallen Christian life? Or is it the Christian shall pray and *the Christian*
shall give life to his friend who has fallen into sin?
Although the latter view might be thought presumptuous
it is the most natural way of taking the Greek and it is
paralleled by statements elsewhere. Paul claimed he had a
ministry that brought life (2 Cor. 2:14-16). He told his
Galatian friends that *they* should restore Christians
overtaken by sin. James tells us that *we* may save a sinner
from death (James 5:19-20). So the idea is that we pray
and God restores the person to spiritual life. The life
certainly comes from God, but the Greek has the idea that
we pray it down for the sinner who needs our help!

(4) John does not want them to be excessively friendly towards the false teachers. His urging them to pray only has in mind 'those who sin but whose sin does not lead to death'. He is not actually asking them to pray for the gnostics who had come into contact with a powerful preaching of the gospel in the ministry of the apostle John, but yet who rejected that message. Almost certainly John has in mind gnostic heretics who have rejected the gospel, when he says **There is a sin which leads to death. I do not say concerning that sin that you should pray** (verse 16b).

It is a word of warning which is without parallel in earlier sections. What is the sin unto death? It has been taken to refer to physical death like the death of Ananias and Sapphira (Acts 5:1-11) or the chastening of 1 Corinthians 11:30. The difficulty with this view is that it does not fit with John's use of life/death terminology. The 'life' that John has just referred to is not physical survival but spiritual restoration. The 'death' must be taken accordingly. There is nothing in 1 John to think that physical chastening to the point of death had come upon any of John's friends. Far from it; 1 John 2:12-14 is his assessment of them. The interpretation of the verse is not so difficult if the actual situation in Ephesus is kept in mind. Obviously this is a very serious sin. What is there in 1 John that it could be referring to?

There is one serious sin mentioned in 1 John, and that is the sin of the gnostics. John has already said that the sins of those who believe the gospel are *not* fatal (1 John 1:7; 2:1-2). And he has said that the sins of the gnostics have been sins against the very heart of the gospel; they are not Christians at all and belong to 'the world'. John's letter has made it clear that the sins of his 'little children' are not sins unto spiritual death. And he has already made it clear that the opposition to the gospel is fatal. John is not being obscure at all. The previous chapters have said enough to make it clear that there are two categories of sin being dealt with in this letter: the lapses of his little children and the much more serious rejection of the gospel on the part of the Gnostic heretics. 1 John 5:16,17 is not parallel to Acts 5:1-11 or 1 Corinthians 11:30. And it is not parallel to the warnings about 'falling away' in Hebrews (which in the context of the letter to the Hebrews deals with God's swearing in wrath such that the Christian loses his inheritance and cannot regain it).

However, there is a similarity between 1 John 5:16,17 and the 'blasphemy against the Spirit' because the reference in both places is to deliberate rejection of Jesus. Only an unbeliever can commit it. One must remember that in Mark 3 we have powerful manifestations of the miracle-power of Jesus (casting out of demons), which is deliberately ascribed by Jesus' enemies to Jesus being the prince of demons (verse 22). This is no ordinary unbelief. It is unbelief in the face of powerful evidences, and it is unbelief in a most vicious and wicked form. It is unforgivable for one reason only: it is rejection of Jesus who is the way of forgiveness. When the Spirit has been powerfully at work it is blasphemy against the Spirit to resist the Spirit's testimony to Jesus.

1 John 5:16b is similar. The gnostics know of John's apostolic message. They have been in the company of Christians (see 2:19), but despite all that they have seen, they reject the gospel. It is a 'sin unto death' only because it refuses to have Jesus, who is the way of forgiveness. It is a sin no Christian has committed or ever can commit. In

any case, no-one need feel alarmed. *No sin is unforgivable except sinning against the means of forgiveness!* John's point is: they don't have to feel obliged to rescue the gnostics. Let them instead rescue their brothers and sisters from the clutches of the gnostics.

(5) He wants them to feel sure about the possibility of restoration. The fact that John is sombre concerning those who have rejected his message must not make the Christians at Ephesus think he is sombre about them. On the other hand, John does not want anyone to feel that because the Christians' sins are 'not unto death' that wrong-doing is harmless. So he says: **¹⁷All unrighteousness is sin, and there is sin which does not lead to death**. His last word in this connection is a word of encouragement, 'There is sin which does not lead to death.' For all sins other than rejecting Jesus he lets them know there is forgiveness!

Questions For Reflection: 1 John 5:6-12

1. What is 'eternal life'?
2. How absolute is God's promise to hear our prayers?
3. How can we be certain God will hear our prayers?

28. Final Affirmations
1 John 5:18-21

1 John 5:18-21 is John's summary of the themes of the letter.

First, Christian faith is not 'sinning religion'; and it gives total security. **[18]We know that everyone who is born of God does not sin**. This recalls 3:6; John's message of fellowship with God by the blood of Christ is encouraging but it does not give easy permission to sin. In this sense the Christian 'does not sin'. The new birth has given him a new nature with a new propensity to love God, and a new ability to love the Christian brotherhood. The Christian has a confidence about his security in the care of Jesus. **The One who is born of God keeps him and the evil one does not get hold of him** (5:18b). There are a number of interpretations of this line, but it is likely that it refers to the ministry of Jesus in protecting His people. The description of Jesus as 'the One who is born of God' is unique, but we have noticed before John's fondness for putting things in unexpected ways. The believer can feel safe because Jesus is able to protect him (see also John 17:11,12,15; 1 Peter 1:5; Jude 24; Rev. 3:10). The converse truth is 'the evil one does not get hold of him'. Satan can attack the believer, entice the believer, trick the believer, deceive the believer – but he cannot remove the believer from Christ's protecting hold.

The second matter which 'we know' is, says John, that he and his disciples authentically hold to the faith, as opposed to the proto-gnostics whose message John refuses to ac-

196

knowledge. **[19]We know that we are of God and the whole world lies in the grasp of the evil one**. One observes again the note of strong affirmation: 'We *know* (without doubt or introspection) that *we* (not the proto-gnostics) *are* (not 'want to be' or 'hope to be') of God'. As distinct to the Christian fellowship, 'the whole world lies in the grasp of the evil one'. There are only two communities in this world: God's people and all others. One is grasped by Jesus, the other is grasped by Satan. Jesus will not loosen His grasp, Satan will not voluntarily loosen his grasp. The Christian is in a situation of conflict against spiritual enemies. The world is *not* in a position of conflict. It is not struggling; it lies almost as though asleep in the grip of Satan.

The third thing which 'we know' follows. **[20]We know also that the Son of God has come and has given to us understanding so that we may know the One who is true, and we are in the One who is true, in His Son Jesus Christ. This is the true God and eternal life**. John is utterly confident that he and his disciples are the authentic heirs of the message of Jesus. His words summarise the gospel over and against the teaching of the heretics. Jesus has come as the Son of God. The Son of God is also the man, 'Jesus' and the divine Saviour, 'Christ'.

John's community who have faith in this Son of God, Jesus Christ, are the true people of God. The anointing of the Spirit has given them faith.

Jesus is 'the One who is true', as opposed to the docetic Christ who is false.

John rises to a great height when he calls Jesus 'God' (see John 1:1; 20:28; Rom. 9:5; Titus 2:13, some of which are disputed). The interpretation is sometimes questioned but is highly likely. It is, in fact, implied by 1 John 5:21. If a false Christ is an idol, the true Christ is God! Verse 21 in itself implies the deity of Christ, and makes good sense after a statement of the deity of Christ.

His last word, **²¹Little children, guard yourselves against idols**, suggests that the second commandment will be 'fulfilled' by the Christian. The second of the ten commandments is subtly touched upon, yet without using a citation formula (such as 'The Scripture says' or the like). There is a delicate indication that the Christian who lives unto Jesus is far from making an idol. A low view of Jesus is idolatry. A true view of Jesus fulfils the second commandment, even without mentioning or focusing on the second commandment.

At this point we can draw a few conclusions about John's first epistle.

John is concerned with the criteria of authentic fellowship among those whose salvation is not in doubt. Our survey has revealed that John is not writing to his adversaries who have left the Johannine community. He is writing to his disciples who have been influenced by his adversaries. John would not believe in the salvation of his adversaries, but he does believe in the salvation of his disciples who accept the testimony of John. He asserts that they are forgiven (1 John 2:12-14); and may be restored if they walk in the light (1:7,9; 2:1-2). They may persuade their hearts that all is well despite the feelings of shame or guilt that they may have in the light of their temptations to proto-gnosticism.

The criterion of true fellowship is three-fold: (i) knowledge of Jesus' incarnate Sonship, (ii) persistence in faith,

(iii) persistent obedience to the commands of love. These criteria are not haphazardly stated. Knowledge of Jesus' incarnate Sonship is prior. There is no possibility of fellowship or righteousness at all if there is no faith in Jesus as the Son of God come in the flesh. Yet even when this prior faith is present, true fellowship with the Father and the Son is not automatic. It comes through 'walking in the light' and 'confessing one's sins'. The love-commands of Jesus must be kept.

The commands of God are mediated to us through Jesus and there are varied manifestations of the love-command. John scarcely makes mention of anything Mosaic. There are allusions (without citation) to three of the ten commandments in his references to lying, murder and idolatry. Yet John obviously interprets 'murder' and 'lying' and 'idolatry' in his own way. At each point his interpretation is Christ-centred. To 'murder' is to fail to live out the love-commands of Jesus. To 'lie' is to deny the incarnation. Idolatry is to have an erroneous portrayal of Jesus. Each command is only delicately mentioned (if one had no previous knowledge of the ten commandments one would never guess that John was citing anything). Each command is only used negatively. Mis-conduct and mis-belief break the stipulations of the Decalogue. Yet John's positive requirements do not quote the Decalogue. They simply summon to a direct faith in Jesus, a direct attention to his love-command.

Unlike Paul, John has no specific concern to urge that the Christian has 'died to the law', yet if we are to evaluate his teaching by taking both his omissions and assertions into account, one's conclusion must be as follows. In John's mind salvation is a matter of knowing by the Spirit

that Jesus is the Righteous One, that he is the Son of God
come in the flesh. The Christian life exhibits minimal interest in the details of Mosaism. The Christian will be concerned not to 'murder' or 'lie' or commit 'idolatry', but
*his interpretation of the requirements of Jesus operates at
an altogether higher level than the requirements of the
Mosaic covenant.* The commands of God will be mediated to him by Jesus. They will come through the Holy
Spirit.

His requirement is that we focus *directly* on Jesus (com-
pare the '*I* say unto you' of the Sermon on the Mount).
Jesus requires love of us. The man or woman who loves
will live rightly. He will not murder or steal or lie. He will
fulfil the law accidentally. Love will act positively in situations of need.

*The Christian is invited to use the requirements of faith
and of love to test everything that claims to be the Christian message.* John wants his disciples to ask: does this
group of teachers present me with Jesus as the Son of God
come in the flesh? Does this lead me to obey Jesus' commands of love?

*There is no introspective element in the thought of 1
John.* John does not want his disciples to ask introspective questions about their own salvation. We are very far
from the 'tests of life' or the 'evidences of grace' that are
characteristic of much evangelicalism of the past as well
as many British Reformed thinkers of the present. It is
enough for John that they 'know that He is the Righteous
One'. This is a *sola fide* ('by faith only') ingredient in
John's thought. However, the fact that he does not invite
introspection does not mean that he does not invite *thought*.
His disciples are to look at the 'Christian' preachers around

them and are to 'test the manifestations of the Spirit' to see that the Johannine tradition *is* right. (John will only put it positively; I cannot write '... to see *whether* the Johannine tradition is right'.) They are to see, by reflection on what has happened to them, that the truth does not lie with the adversaries of John who have parted company with the original community. John has no doubt that if they reflect they will see that 'we' (the Johannine disciples) *are* from God. If they discern that Jesus is the Righteous One, they will *also* discern who are and who are not the righteous ones. John calls them to continuance in faith in Jesus, a simple certainty concerning Jesus' coming in the flesh, a single-minded adherence to the plural-yet-single command of Jesus to abide in love.

Questions For Reflection: 1 John 5:18-21

1. Can the modern Christian be an idolater?
2. What are the tests of true fellowship with God?
3. How can fellowship with God be lost? What can be done about it?

2 JOHN

29. Reward Protected
2 John 1-8

2 and 3 John are the two shortest books of the New Testament. 2 John has in view the same kind of situation that gave rise to 1 John, and one can detect the same heresy in the background. In 3 John the problem being faced is not heresy but needless divisiveness.

Almost every scholar agrees that the author of 2 and 3 John was the same as the author of 1 John. If John the apostle wrote 1 John (as I have suggested), he also wrote 2 and 3 John.

2 John was written to a congregation; 3 John was written to an individual. 2 John deals with restricting fellowship and recognition to those who maintain the gospel. 3 John deals with embracing in fellowship and welcoming in ministry all who hold the gospel of Jesus. 2 John refuses to welcome heretics; 3 John insists on welcoming brothers. 2 John needs to be pondered by those who compromise the gospel; 3 John needs to be pondered by those who are power-hungry and will not compromise on anything!

In 2 John we have an introduction (1-3), a central section (4-11) and a farewell (12-13).

First is the introduction. **¹The elder to the elect lady and her children, whom I love in the truth, and not I only but all who know the truth, ²because of the truth which remains in us and will be with us for ever. ³Grace, mercy and peace will be with us, from God the Father and from Jesus Christ, the Son of the Father, in truth and love**. Presumably John called himself 'the elder' because that was one of the ways in which he was known in the area of Ephesus.

(1) *John's very style of writing reflects his friendly ways.*
'The elder' is a pleasant, gentle, humble term. The ones
receiving the letter are 'the elect lady and her children'.
This is a playful and friendly way of referring to a congregation. The word 'you' is at first singular ('I am asking
you, lady ...'), but it soon becomes plural ('... This is the
command, as you heard ... that you walk in love ... Look to
yourselves that you do not lose what you have worked for
...' and so on). In verse 13 the 'you' is singular again. The
'elect lady' is a plurality, a church.

John's very style is a study in truth and love. He uses
amusing and pleasant language, and although he has severe things to say (in 7-11), he combines his firmness with
an enjoyable, lovable style.

(2) *He expresses his love,* assuring the 'elect lady' and her
children (that is, the congregation), that he loves them 'in
the truth' (that is, genuinely and in the truth of the gospel). Many Christians are afraid to convey love in the way
they do things. They feel they might be thought weak, or
they might be taken advantage of, or they are afraid to
share their feelings. Perhaps they are too proud or they
feel that if they express affection they will be making themselves too vulnerable. John has none of these fears and
tells these Christian friends how much he loves them.

(3) *He roots love in the gospel.* He loves them all 'in the
truth'; others who 'know the truth' also love them dearly
(verse 1). And he says the love that the Christians have for
this congregation is 'because of the truth *which remains
in us and will be with us for ever*'.

The phrase 'the truth which ... will be with us for ever'

is something he has not said anywhere else in these let-ters. In the Old Testament it was promised that David's seed, which ultimately is Jesus, would endure for ever (Psalm 89:36-37). John's gospel tells us the Son of God would endure for ever (John 8:35; 12:34). In 1 John we have been told that the person who does God's will will live for ever (2:17). A person who keeps Jesus' word does not see death – ever (John 8:51). The truth that generates love for all of God's people is a truth that has permanence. Love will go on for ever. The Christian comes into an eternal kingdom of love.

When the entire planet earth is demolished and rebuilt, what will survive is the kingdom of love. Jesus will last for ever; his people will last for ever; love will last for ever. Everything will radiate with love in the new heavens and new earth. All enmities and hostilities will be at an end, and all the inhabitants of glory will endlessly be a people of love. In this confidence, the Christian 'remains' in the truth. He stays there, and applies the truth in his life. He lives in fellowship with God, and walks in the light. The result is *lasting* change, which begins now and lasts for ever, a change in the direction of love.

(4) John's greeting is part of the same friendliness of the gospel. *Grace, mercy and peace will be with us, from God the Father and Jesus Christ, the Son of the Father, in truth and love* (verse 4). These words are a confident affirma-tion. Despite testings, heresies and internal strife, John is confident that his churches will experience God's grace (His help to the helpless), God's mercy (His kindness to the guilty), God's peace (His comfort for the alienated).

Verse 4 brings John to the main burden of what he wants

to say. He is concerned about love and truth. He begins with love and glides into remarks about truth. As always he is concerned with *living* the truth. The truth when put into practice turns out as love. And that in turn leads to joy. There are five points I want to look at arising from verses 4-8.

(1) John commends the church for truth-turned-into-love, encourages them to continue in the way that they have been living, and reminds them that it is an obligatory way of living, a 'command from the Father'. **⁴I rejoiced greatly because I found some of your children walking in the truth just as we received command from the Father**.

(2) His commendation turns into exhortation. **⁵And now I am asking you, lady, not as someone writing a new command but one which we received from the beginning, that we love one another**. Love is the permanent and long-intended design of the Father. It is what the Father has always been seeking since the origin of sin in the human race.

(3) His request relates love to commands. Love is not fully able to be put into legislation, yet neither is it undefined. It is able to be put into words, able to be expressed as commands. **⁶And this is love, that we walk according to His commands. This is the command, as you heard from the beginning; it is that you walk in love**.

(4) Verse 7 introduces the warning concerning heresy: **Because many deceivers have gone out into the world, who do not confess Jesus Christ as the One who came in the flesh. Such a one is the deceiver and Antichrist**. Although

John's concern is love, it requires truth to get to love! The precise thread of the argument at this point is important. John does not speak of false *teaching* in verses 1-6, but about love. He does not say 'This *teaching* is commanded, because there are many deceivers...'. Instead he says 'This is the command ... walk in love, because there are many deceivers...'. The precise logic of what he says should be noticed. He does not raise the matter of false doctrine at first. What he raises is lovelessness. The question of love-lessness is what leads into a warning about the truth. When John gets to his warning about anti-incarnational heresy it is in order to produce a people of love. Where there is no faith in Jesus Christ as the One who has come in the flesh, the end-product will be lovelessness. He warns about the substitutes for Jesus that seek to impose themselves on the Christian churches. But his concern is not doctrine for its own sake. His concern is that God should have a peo-ple of love in this world. 'The truth' is the way of getting there.

(5) Lack of truth leads to lack of love which in turn leads to loss of reward. **⁸Look to yourselves that you do not lose what you have worked for, but receive a full reward**. It is interesting that John brings in the theme of reward. Many Christians find it difficult to accept the idea of living for reward. Yet Jesus constantly spoke of reward, and it is not possible to be more spiritual than Jesus (see Matthew 5:12; 6:4, 6, 18; 10:41, 42; 16:27, and the concept of 'inherit-ing' throughout the gospels). It perhaps helps us too if we remember that the reward is not at all commercial; it is itself a spiritual matter. It is not 'mercenary' to want spir-itual blessings from Jesus.

Elsewhere John spoke of the security of the Christian in salvation. 'His seed remains in him ... he is born of God' (1 John 3:9). The new birth is permanent. The new birth is never lost, but reward can be lost. Reward comes through living the life of love and achieving something for God in this world. False teachers can damage our fellowship, undo the work we have done, and bring about loss of reward.

What is the reward? John does not say. Because it is not possible to know completely, we can only think of it in terms of picture-language. Yet it includes visible honour, a visible level of glory. It involves the 'well done' of Jesus. It is our contribution to the kingdom of God becoming known. John's concern is that if we dabble with gnosticism our contribution to the kingdom of God will be nil. Being 'rewarded fully' involves living a life of love, and that in turn involves walking in the truth, the truth of the gospel of the incarnate Son of God.

Questions For Reflection: 2 John 1-8

1. Do you find John to be a good example of love?
2. Do some people find it easier to show love than others?
3. How do we balance love and teaching?

30. False Progress
2 John 9-13

The central concern of 2 John is to be found in verses 4-11. There are two essential commands for the Christian (4-5). Love is vital (6), but John is expounding his concern for truth as a means of getting to love (7-11). He has spoken of his concern that the Christians do not lose reward (7-8). Now he comes to another aspect of the matter.

(1) There is a danger of false 'progressiveness'. **⁹Everyone who goes ahead and does not remain in the teaching of Christ does not have God.** Of course every Christian should want to 'go ahead' with God. Yet there is a hazard of being 'progressive' beyond the bounds of revelation. The apostolic revelation (now in our New Testament) requires progressive obedience, progressive application, progressive understanding. But it is not possible to 'progress' beyond the doctrine of the incarnation!

(2) It is 'remaining' in the teaching that leads to fellowship with God. **He who remains in the teaching has both the Father and the Son** (verse 9b). If the Christian welcomes the 'new theology' of the gnostics at Ephesus he will find himself damaging his fellowship with God. The gnostics have no fellowship with God at all; any Christian who listens to them approvingly will find his own fellowship with God is damaged. If we wish to 'have' God, to know Him, to have Him give us spiritual power, to be used by Him in His service, it is necessary to 'remain in the teaching'.

(3) 'Progressiveness' that wanders from the centralities of
the faith forfeits the right to be called 'Christian'. **¹⁰If any
one comes to you and does not bring this teaching, do not
receive him into the house or give him any greeting.**

The details of this warning should be noted.

(i) John refers to official teachers. 'If anyone comes...'.
Clearly visiting teachers claiming to be Christians are what
John has in mind.

(ii) He is concerned about missing ingredients in the
teaching. 'If any one comes to you and does *not* bring this
teaching...'. It is not so much what the false teachers say;
it is more a matter of what they leave out. It has been said
that 'subtraction from the truth is something that members of churches are very, very slow to observe'.[1] False
teachers know how to say what their orthodox listeners
will like, and simply leave out certain matters! But if the
false teacher goes on teaching long enough it becomes
noticeable (if one is not naive) that certain essential matters are left out. John says to his friends, 'If you do not
hear them talking about the Son of God come in the flesh',
take note of the omission!

(iii) John asks that the false teachers should be refused
hospitality as visiting religious teachers. 'Do not receive
him into the house.'

(iv) John asks that such a person should not be treated
with such marks of approval that it might seem that his
message is being approved. 'Do not give him any greeting.'

(v) John urges that there is a danger of sincerely but
misguidedly doing great harm. Do not greet him, says John
... **¹¹for he who greets him is a sharer in his wicked works**.

---

1. D. M. Lloyd-Jones, *Knowing the Times* (Banner of Truth, 1989), p.
320.

FALSE PROGRESS213

It is important for the modern Christian to notice precisely what is and what is not at stake at this point. There
are certain matters in the Christian faith that are non-
negotiable, but there are other matters which call for a lot
of tolerance.

When, for example, Paul is discussing   vegetarian-
ism and the keeping of (presumably) Jewish special days
on the calendar, he is able to say 'Let each person be convinced in (or "by") his own mind' (Rom. 14:5). In writing
to the Corinthians he speaks of his flexibility in such matters: 'To the Jews I became as a Jew ... To those outside
the law I became as outside the law ... To the weak I became weak ... I have become all things to all men, that I
might by all means save some' (1 Cor. 9:21-23). There
were areas where Paul would say 'The person that is weak
in the faith, you should receive ...' (Rom. 14:1).

Yet clearly there are other aspects of the Christian faith
that are decidedly non-negotiable, and where the attitude
of the apostles is more unyielding. The question is: is there
any way of deciding what parts of the gospel of Jesus Christ
are non-negotiable and utterly indispensable to salvation?

In 1 and 2 John the issue is the incarnation of the Son
of God. John did not issue the severe warning of 2 John
10-11 when talking about modes of baptism, or views of
the millennium, or styles of church government, or minor
matters of conduct. He was talking about a much bigger
matter: the Son of God taking human flesh.

Within the New Testament we find stern admonitions
not to depart from the message that has been preached
(Gal. 1:6-9), nor to extend hospitality to one who 'goes
ahead' – that is ahead of the apostolic norm – 'and does
not abide in the doctrine of Christ' (2 John 9, 10).

What is included in the non-negotiable? It certainly includes the following five points:

(i) The authority of the first generation of apostles. 'If anyone thinks he is a prophet ... he should acknowledge that what I am writing is of the Lord. If anyone does not recognise this, he is not recognised' (1 Cor. 14:37-38).

(ii) The main facts of the gospel are also central. What was at stake when John uttered his stern words in 2 John 10,11 was the reality of the incarnation. Similar statements are made about the reality of the resurrection and the second coming of Jesus.

(iii) The reality of sin is the issue that lies behind the admonitions of 2 Peter and Jude.

(iv) The person of God and the reality of the supernatural are on a similar level.

(v) The nature of salvation by grace is of vital importance. This is the theme of Galatians with its warning in Galatians 1:6-9.

These areas are clearly treated as non-negotiable by the New Testament writers. False teaching here would be grounds for discipline or withdrawal, grounds for excluding certain religious teachers or if necessary restarting the church. These are the kinds of teaching that are essential to the church. Any who disagree with these matters are not believers in the gospel message at all.

Wicked living is similarly of great significance. Christians must live a holy life. When professing Christians fall into major sin, the church must not act in such a way that it seems that the church agrees with such sin. In as loving a way as possible, the church must disassociate herself from sin.

Spiritual deadness also may require strong action. The church must stay alive with the living energy of the Holy Spirit.

The Christian holds the truth, or is held by the truth; he is alive unto God; he lives the life of godliness. These things are essential to authentic Christianity. Any congregation which is not right here is useless. True Christians must either reform it or find a way to restart the preaching of the authentic gospel.

In the various parts of the world the gospel must be 'contextualised' (made appropriate to the local situation) with great care. Each nation will want to express the gospel in a way that fits the local situation, but it must be remembered that the desire to make Christianity indigenous has not always been matched with the power of discernment with regard to false teaching. John makes it starkly clear that anti-incarnational heresy must receive no recognition or support. There can be no 'localised' gospel at this point.

Admittedly, true Christians do not always agree about peripheral matters of Christian doctrine and life. Even in some very vital matters, such as the interpretation of the work of the Holy Spirit or one's doctrine of sanctification, Christians may have to be patient with one another. But there is a 'hard core' of Christian faith that is entirely non-negotiable. John Calvin wrote: 'Not all the articles of true doctrine are of the same sort.'[2] Let us make sure we can draw the distinction between errors that destroy the gospel and those that do not.

In a few closing lines (verses 12-13) John again reveals

---

2. Calvin: *Institutes of the Christian Religion* (SCM, 1961), vol. 2, p. 1025.

his magnanimity and gentleness. He puts personal contact above pen and ink: **12I have many things to write to
you, but I do not wish just to use paper and black ink.
Instead, I hope to come to you and talk with you face to
face, so that our joy may be full.** Here is a man who wants
to maintain joy in his life. In a friendly way he gives the
greeting of the church where he is currently residing, **13The
children of your elect sister greet you.** Truth and love flow
together to the very end. John prefers personal contact to
written contact. This is a vital aspect of the gospel. Christian faith must not be 'bookish', not even with respect to
the inspired Scriptures. John preferred personal contact
above writing some more of the Bible! Of course he did
not quite envisage our modern Bibles, but he knew he was
writing with authority. Yet he put his desire for personal
face-to-face fellowship above his desire to do some more
writing.

No matter how much writing we may read – including
these expositions of mine – it is only a form of back-up to
the living power of the Holy Spirit, in living person-with-
person situations. God's salvation comes by speaking more
than by writing, by hearing more than by reading, by people more than by books. We are children of Abraham and
Abraham never wrote a book and perhaps never read one
either! The law of Moses was in written form from its first
day, but the restructured people of God, the church of
Jesus Christ, did not have the New Testament from the
first day. They had the Holy Spirit. And when the New
Testament was finally written it did not replace the Holy
Spirit. John is writing a little bit of the New Testament, but
he wants something additional! He wants to sit down with
his brothers and sisters and have the Holy Spirit working

among them, as they enjoy fellowship with the Father, fellowship with the Son, fellowship with one another.

Questions For Reflection: 2 John 9-13

1. Can we be 'progressive' in understanding God's truth?
2. Is John's instruction too harsh?
3. Can one obey John's instruction and still show love?

3 JOHN

31. Hospitality
(3 John 1-8)

In 3 John we have an introduction (verse 1) and an expression of joy (verses 2-4). Then we have the central section which considers three people, Gaius (verses 5-8), Diotrophes (verses 9-11) and Demetrius (verse 12). Finally John makes some concluding remarks (verses 13-15).

¹The elder to the beloved Gaius, whom I love in the truth. ²Beloved, I pray that you may prosper in all things and be in health, just as your soul prospers. ³For I greatly rejoiced when the brothers came and bore witness about you in the truth, just as you are walking in the truth. ⁴I have no greater joy than this, to hear that my children are walking in the truth.

We catch a glimpse here of an early Christian fellowship. First, there is John himself, who again calls himself 'the elder'; it is a gentle, tactful, humble title. John is a man of humility who does not needlessly come across in a heavy way to his friend Gaius. He is a man of open love. He expresses his affection. He is a man of joy, and expresses his rejoicing in God and in God's people.

A second character is 'Gaius'. He is a member of the church (or churches) to which John writes. He is much loved by John himself (verses 1-2), and loyal to the gospel. John loves him 'in truth', which means 'truly'; but it also means 'in the truth' or 'in the gospel of Jesus'. Gaius believes the truth and he works it out in his life. He 'walks' (practises) the truth.

Thirdly, there is mention of 'the brothers' who came and told their story about Gaius. There is contact between John and Gaius by means of travelling Christians. Gaius' church was evidently directed by John. They are 'his children' (verse 4).

These words create a picture of a loving community. Love arises especially between those who have a common Saviour. Love needs to be genuine and fearless. There must be a determination to continue in a good relationship no matter what hindrances might be faced. It must be love like the love between David and Jonathan whose friendship was open, generous and covenanted. Love that refused jealousy.

One bond of love between these people is prayer. John prays for his friend Gaius and tells him of the things he is praying for him. 'I pray that you may prosper in all things and be in health, just as your soul prospers.'

It is an interesting prayer, and one that has sometimes been over-pressed by the 'health and wealth' sub-section of the charismatic movement. It has sometimes been taken that material and earthly prosperity is promised to all Christians. Such prosperity is seen in terms of prestigious employment, being 'the head and not the tail', ample financial provision. 'See,' it is said, 'John urges prosperity in every respect and especially mentions health. Also John puts it on a level with spiritual health. So it is just as much God's will that we have physical and financial prosperity as it is that our souls prosper.'

Such teaching is mistaken, but before we run too quickly to point out its mistakes, its strong points should be noted. In favour of our 'health and wealth' friends – and they are friends not enemies – it must be said that they are reacting to a weakness in the church that was present before their movement arose. In days gone by, there was too much unbelief in such matters, too much consulting of doctors before we consult God at all! There was too much 'if it be Thy will' type of praying. It is not surprising that an extremist movement should arise in the church. There was such weakness in the faith of the 'orthodox', that it was inevitable that a reaction should set in and go too far in the other direction.

Our friends are right to note that John includes such practical matters as prosperity and health in his praying. Many would think that too earthly, but not John.

However, there are some things that ought to caution us against pressing this verse too far. This prayer like all other prayers is subject to the sovereignty of God. There is much teaching in Scripture about the place of hardship and suffering, and of finding strength in weakness. Our friends make rather too much use of the Old Testament where wealth and prosperity are more prominent. How many rich Christians are there in the New Testament? A few, but 'not many' (1 Cor. 1:26; see also James 2:5). There seem also to be clear cases where Christians are sick, and healing is not regarded as automatic or as absolutely guaranteed (Phil. 2:25-27; 1 Tim. 5:23). All of this should hold us back from going all the way with our 'health and wealth' friends. We should admit that they have something to teach us, that their faith is often honoured by God, that their emphasis corrects an unbelief in older circles of Christian faith and living. But in the final analysis 'health and wealth' is a deviation; the gospel puts its emphasis on salvation from sin, says we are *waiting* for the redemption of the body and holds out no guarantee of wealth beyond the needs of the calling God has put us in. We pray for prosperity in all things and for health. God often answers us with exactly what we have in mind, but our entire situation stays under

His will. We do not 'name it and claim it' as though we
were already kings of the universe. That is what we shall
be. That is the glory that is on its way, but we have not
quite reached glory yet! Meanwhile we do what John did;
we pray and God will meet all our needs, but perhaps not
all our greeds.

Verses 5-12 bring us to the central section of the letter.
There is encouragement for Gaius (verses 5-8), concern
about Diotrophes (verses 9-11) and commendation of
Demetrius (verse 12).

**⁵Beloved, you are showing faithfulness when you are at
work on behalf of the brothers and sisters, especially when
they are strangers to you...** Apparently Gaius and his friends
would often help travelling Christians who were not known
to them personally, receiving them as a way of helping
them in the work of God. John continues **⁶They have given
witness about your love before the congregation** (i.e. the
congregation where John is at present staying). **You will
do well if you help them forward on their journey in a way
that is worthy of God. ⁷For they went out in service towards
the Name, taking nothing from the Gentiles.** These travelling Christian workers ventured forth simply to spread the
message concerning Jesus and to bring honour to His name.
They had taken no financial support from their pagan
neighbours and friends. John is commending the way in
which Gaius and his friends have cared for and given warm
hospitality to the travelling workers. He wants it to continue. **⁸For this reason we ought to support such people, in
order to be fellow-workers for the truth.**

Hospitality is a vital matter if the gospel of Jesus is to
go forward. It is not enough to have 'missionary' organisations and guest houses and hotels. There will always be

need, if the church of God is truly alive with the vibrancy of the Holy Spirit, to have travelling preachers, and that implies the need of hospitality. It is one of the themes of the New Testament (Rom. 12:13; Heb. 13:2; 1 Tim. 3:2; 5:10; Titus 1:8).

John gives six reasons for such hospitality.

(i) Loyalty to the Lord: 'Beloved, you are showing faithfulness...'.

(ii) Christian love: 'You are ... at work on behalf of the brothers and sisters ... They have given witness about your love...'.

(iii) Hospitality is a way of showing how great the love of our God is: 'Help them ... in a way that is worthy of God.'

(iv) Hospitality shows concern for the honour of Jesus. The travelling workers went out 'in service towards the Name', so the Christians with Gaius should do the same thing in showing concern for the honour of Jesus.

(v) Christians should not have to rely on worldly support. They had gone out 'taking nothing from the Gentiles'. John uses emphatic words when he says 'For this reason *we* ought to support such people ...'.

(vi) Christians who are not travellers in the work of the gospel desire to be involved in it and to receive the blessings and rewards for such involvement. John urges them to be 'fellow-workers for the truth'.

We have seen the warnings of 2 John about not showing hospitality to false teachers, but there is another side to the matter. True servants of God should be warmly received and helped. John envisages situations where strangers arrive, yet soon they are no longer strangers but friends. Whenever there is the liveliness of the Holy Spirit this situation arises again and again. When the church becomes cold and traditional there is not so much need for hospitality, but when God is at work and things are happening it is different. Emergencies arise. Unexpected people come to salvation some distance away. A need arises in this area or that area that is so great that Christians have to be sent speedily to give help. A burst of revival takes place here and another there. It is nothing to have half a dozen Christian friends arrive from a church a hundred miles away to teach the new converts how to pray, how to witness. In a situation of liveliness and blessing, impromptu hospitality becomes the need of the hour. Food has to be produced at a moment's notice. Beds and blankets have to be found. Christian neighbours have to be visited. 'I am taking four of them. Do you have any room ...? Can you lend me some bread ...?' What blessings it brings, and sometimes 'angels unawares' (Heb. 13:2)!

Questions For Reflection: 3 John 1-8

1. Is 'hospitality' a spiritual gift?
2. Is 'hospitality' needed today?
3. How 'earthly' should we expect God's blessings to be?

32. Conflicts in the Church
3 John 9-14

The hospitality that had been shown to travelling Christians was disliked by a man named Diotrophes. **⁹I wrote something to the church, says John, but Diotrophes, that person who loves to have an eminent position over the church does not receive us.** Apparently Diotrophes had not even allowed the church to get the letter, and this is why John is now writing to Gaius.

Diotrophes had a personality disorder that had not been corrected and that was now damaging the fellowship of the Christians. We do not become perfect Christians the day after we are saved, not even by the next weekend! Diotrophes had a problem. Despite his being a Christian, there was a serious problem that had arisen in the church because of his personality difficulty. We all have personality difficulties. I sometimes say when I am preaching, 'If you have no personality problems in your life, please come and see me afterwards and shake me by the hand. I might get some of your anointing!'

Diotrophes was not causing trouble in the church because he was like the people of 2 John 10. He had a perfectly orthodox gospel, but his problem was that it was not being applied to his own personality. It is like that with all of us! We have our particular strengths and weaknesses. Actually our strengths and our weaknesses are often the same thing. What from one point of view is a strength, from another point of view is a weakness. One type of person knows what he wants, thinks with great lucidity and has great drive in getting things done. Perhaps Diotrophes was like that! Yet such a person wants

227

to do things in his own way, gets upset when visiting preachers arrive, and wants to keep others out of leadership positions, the apostle John included!

John's teaching about not receiving false teachers was one matter. But proud separatism is another. Diotrophes wanted to be a separatist. What were his reasons? It was not a matter of false teaching on this occasion. John and the travelling Christian workers were not heretics and John does not accuse Diotrophes of being a heretic. Was it a disagreement where the best thing was to 'agree to disagree'? Not so far as we know. It was simply that Diotrophes desired to have the pre-eminence. He wanted to be in a prominent position and did not care who he put down to stay on top, even the apostle John! John was rather elderly. Perhaps Diotrophes was saying, 'John ought to step down from his apostolic position and give way to a younger man.' Perhaps he was building his own empire and wanting to be leader in the Ephesian area. The fact that John has suggested that financial help be given to these travelling workers (verses 7, 8) suggests that this too might have been a problem to Diotrophes. People who want an eminent position normally want an eminent salary too; it is probable that Diotrophes disliked the help being given to meet the needs of others.

There are times when it is necessary to refuse hospitality. John mentions such times elsewhere (2 John). Heresy is a ground for refusing so-called 'fellowship' (it would not be 'fellowship' anyway!). There are also times when Christians have to 'agree to differ'. The model here is Paul and Barnabas (Acts 15:39). They had a strong disagreement. It was a sad business, but I have no doubt that they made the right decision when they decided to go their separate ways and allow each to develop his own ministry. But even then there is good reason to think they retained fellowship, and Mark became Paul's companion again in later years (2 Tim. 4:11).

But Diotrophes is a case of 'schism', an unjustifiable breach of fellowship between people who hold firmly to the gospel of Jesus. Diotrophes resisted the authority of the apostle (verse 9), slandered the apostle (verse 10a), roused opposition against him and disciplined those who would not submit to his views (verse 10b).

What does John do?

(1) He asserts apostolic authority. He might be John 'the old man' (verse 1), but he can also say 'Therefore, if I come I will call attention to the things he is doing...' John clearly intends to take hold firmly of the leadership once again.

(2) John will bring all the facts to light. **¹⁰Therefore, if I come I will call attention to the things he is doing, and his unjustly speaking against us with evil words. Not satisfied with these things, also he does not receive the brothers and he forbids those who want to do so and he puts them out of the churches**. John might be the 'apostle of love', but he can combine love with strength.

(3) John gives Diotrophes an opportunity to repent. By sending an official letter via Gaius, supporting the bulk of the church, and by warning of his possible arrival, John is giving Diotrophes a chance to back down before he comes. His firmness is not so great that he instructs Diotrophes to be put out of the church. He is to be left alone for the

moment. The church must regain its hospitality, Diotrophes
must change his ways. But John does leave time for all of
this to happen. Wise man!

(4) John takes the opportunity to press home his oft-re-
peated teaching concerning the outworking of the Christian gospel. The Christian is in a position where he must
freely apply what he knows in the way he lives. John has
put a good example to them; they must not copy Diotrophes. **¹¹Beloved, do not imitate what is evil but what is
good**. The origin of godly love is the knowledge of God:
The well-doer is of God. The evil-doer has not seen God
(verse 11b). This means that the way in which one shows
hospitality or withholds hospitality is an indicator as to
whether right now the person is or is not walking closely
with God. Salvation is not at issue here. John says not a
word to question Diotrophes' salvation, but he does raise
a question about whether such actions arise from 'seeing
God'.

Perhaps by the time John gets to Gaius' congregation
Diotrophes will climb down. John might be able to get
close to him. At this time when he is writing his letter he
is not trying to get close to Diotrophes; he is trying to
rescue the church and keep the work of God going. This is
what pastors spend much of their time doing! But maybe
when he gets there he will be able to help Diotrophes. He
will speak lovingly to him about the cleansing blood of
Christ. He will get Diotrophes to listen. He will let
Diotrophes talk and tell John the way he feels about the
life of the church and what needs to be done. Maybe John
will tell Diotrophes about the time when he wanted to call
thunder down on some Samaritans and Jesus had to re-

buke him and tell him that that was not the way to do God's work.

But all of that will have to wait. Right now John must put the needs of the church above the needs of one person. Diotrophes is firmly put down and Demetrius is firmly supported.

It is this that John now moves to. He must say a word about Demetrius, another person in the church. **¹²Demetrius**, says John, **has received a good testimonial from everyone and from the truth itself. And we also bear witness, as you know that our testimony is true**. Some think that Demetrius is a missionary being sent to Gaius' church, but the similarity to verse 4 suggests that Demetrius is within Gaius' church and that John wants him to have more influence there. People ought to come into prominence in the church, not by their own manipulations, but by steadily winning a good recommendation by their pastoral skill. Demetrius has three testimonials: John himself recommends him; the Christians who have observed him all speak well of him; and his own way of life flowing from his living the truth speaks for itself.

Finally John says: **¹³I have many things to write to you, but I do not wish to use just black ink and a pen**. John is no longer one of the young and inexperienced 'sons of thunder' that half a century before wanted to call down fire upon the Samaritans to consume them (Luke 9:54). He puts personal contact high on his agenda. He loves people more than he loves writing and reading. I sometimes say to my friends, 'When I was a youngster, I loved books, but I have learned to love people more than I love books.' John would have liked to hear that! He says, **¹⁴On the contrary I am hoping to see you soon, and we shall talk face to face**.

Although he is a man of strength and can say very firm things about false teaching (2 John) and false living (3 John), he is fundamentally a man of peace and a lover of people. Verse 14b – some translations call it verse 15 – expresses his deepest concerns. **Peace be with you. The friends greet you. Greet our friends by name**. These are the things that concern John: peace, fraternity, continued contact and involvement with Christian people, love expressed in friendship given and friendship received. He wants to maintain love and peace among his friends and stay in touch with them 'one by one' (as the New English Bible has it). It is this that expresses the gospel; this is what it means to 'walk in the truth'. It is a foretaste of heaven; fellowship with the Father, fellowship with the Son, fellowship given by the Spirit, fellowship among God's people. It is this concerning which John says there is 'no greater joy'.

Questions For Reflection: 3 John 9-14

1. Was Diotrophes a Christian?
2. Can a Christian have a personality disorder?
3. What is the biggest impact upon your life that has come through 1, 2 and 3 John?

Below are listed available and forthcoming volumes in the Focus on the Bible Commentary Series. Those available in 1996 are marked by an asterisk. Other volumes are in early stages of preparation.

The whole Bible should be completed by 2001.

Authors in the series are selected from different countries and denominations. Each is committed to the explanation of the Word of God and its application to the world today.

Exodus: John L Mackay
Judges and Ruth: Stephen Dray
1 and 2 Samuel: David Searle
1 and 2 Chronicles: Richard Pratt*
Ezra, Nehemiah and Esther: John Armstrong
Psalms: Allan Harman
Daniel: Robert Fyall
Hosea: Michael Eaton
Jonah, Micah, Nahum: John L Mackay*
Habbukkuk and Zephaniah: John L Mackay
Haggai, Zechariah and Malachi: John L Mackay*
Matthew: Charles Price
Mark: Geoffrey Grogan*
John: Steve Motyer
Acts: Ron Davies
Romans: R C Sproul*
2 Corinthians: Geoffrey Grogan*

Ephesians: R. C. Sproul*
Philippians: Hywel Jones*
1 and 2 Thessalonians: David Jackman
1 and 2 Timothy and Titus: Douglas Milne*
Hebrews: Walter Riggans
1, 2, 3 John: Michael Eaton*
Revelation: Steve Motyer